Angela Ambrosia

ANGELA AMBROSIA

by Ray Errol Fox

Alfred A. Knopf   New York   1979

THIS IS A BORZOI BOOK
PUBLISHED BY ALFRED A. KNOPF, INC.

Copyright © 1979 by Ray Errol Fox and A. A. Rubel. All
rights reserved under International and Pan-American
Copyright Conventions. Published in the United States by
Alfred A. Knopf, Inc., New York, and simultaneously in
Canada by Random House of Canada Limited, Toronto.
Distributed by Random House, Inc., New York.

Manufactured in the United States of America
FIRST EDITION

Library of Congress Cataloging in Publication Data
Fox, Ray Errol.   Angela Ambrosia.

1. Leukemia—Biography.   2. Rubel, Angela Ambrosia.
I. Title.
RC643.F67   1979   362.1 '9 615509   78-20386
ISBN 0-394-50096-2

For Jean B. and Jean T.

Thank You —

Laurie Praver and Amanda Able, who brought
Angela and me together; Joan Hyler and Betty Anne
Clarke, who brought concept and reality together;
Robert Gottlieb and Charles Elliott, who brought the
book together; Amy Krugman and Elizabeth
Catenaccio, who brought the pages together; Joe V.
and Julie C.; Monroe D. Dowling, M.D.; Jay S. Harris
and Susan F. Schulman, who are always there for
me; Ted, who was never there until he was needed;
and Lauren and Haley, who were very patient with
me.

R.E.F.

Angela Ambrosia

"I don't ever remember being well." This is the way Angela introduced her life to me.

By the time she was sixteen, she had grown accustomed to feeling disliked, and being disliked, for spoiling everyone else's fun. Since the age of thirteen, she had persistently complained of sore throats and pains in her groin. She was always tired, couldn't keep up with anyone—"lazy," they said. In the dark ages of her infirmity she was blamed for the routinely canceled outings and scolded for the feelings of inadequacy she created in those around her. Pain suppressed became pain unbearable. Family and friends who sought to cure by yelling only succeeded in making her more and more self-conscious. Swollen glands, though unobserved by others, distort the self-image. Particularly in an adolescent. So does losing friends—when identifying with the pack is so vital—because other sixteen-year-olds don't trust one who always listens to her mother, a "mama's

3

girl." Which she was, because a young girl turns to Mama when something is wrong, and she *knew* something was wrong.

Her mother wasn't so quick to know. But she was quick to defend when her daughter was accused of making her sister-in-law's daughter ill. Angela was rushed to the family doctor for blood tests and no sooner was she cleared of the charge—of carrying mononucleosis—than a second call came from the doctor, "We don't know what it is, but separate all her dishes and silver from the rest of the family's," and a third, the only explanation available at the moment, "We haven't seen anything like this for a long time." Blood test followed blood test, until a bone-marrow extraction was required. The doctor extracting the marrow was more intent on answering his phones and his door than on being attentive to a sixteen-year-old girl who had to have her sternum cracked to admit the upright needle between her breasts. "I can feel my spine and shoulder bones being sucked out through the syringe," she rasped, and went into shock. The result of this crudely administered test was days and nights of nightmarish reaction from which she in due course recovered, but which produced a diagnosis from which she could never recover. She wasn't told—she was never to be told—she had six months to live.

You can't blame the family doctor for despairing of a cure. This was 1968 and leukemia didn't respond to treatment. But her family didn't want to know that. Her sister's husband, Tony, sought the advice of an ex-professor of his who was a physician and who

4

urged Tony to take her to Dr. Monroe Dowling at Manhattan's Memorial Sloan-Kettering Cancer Center. Doctor and hospital were three trains and at least as many worlds away from Angela's parochial Brooklyn neighborhood and her Italian Catholic upbringing. She had never been asked to undress fully for a doctor before. Now she stood before a tall, light-skinned black, hoping that this awesome stranger could tell her what was wrong with her. She was so lonely, so isolated in her infirmity, that when he asked her some embarrassing questions he had forewarned her he must ask, she was flattered because such unaccustomed intimacy about her person and her habits made her feel "more normal."

Putting oneself in the hands of a doctor is always a complicated matter. He's supposed to find something wrong, but not too wrong—not as wrong as things were with Angela. The first doctor had found a white cell count of 50,000, five to ten times the rate of a normal count; the second doctor had found that the bone marrow, "the blood factory," was producing abnormal cells. Their diagnosis of chronic myelogenous leukemia, an infrequent blood disease more common among middle-aged males, was clinically correct. But at Memorial her white cell count tested at 14,000; and Dr. Dowling was dissatisfied because her first bone-marrow sample had not been tested for the presence of an enigmatic chromosome known as the Philadelphia chromosome. This fragment of genetic tissue, the exact role of which in leukemia remains a mystery, is nevertheless present in many leukemic cases and thus presents a strong determining factor. While

Angela craved any explanation for feeling as she did, and her parents harbored the secret of why she felt that way and prayed for a miracle, Dowling could neither confirm nor refute the diagnosis without repeating the bone-marrow test. The Ambrosias were distressed, certain Angela would be "impossible." Dowling promised it would be different, and thought the thing to do was to explain the entire situation to her. But they were adamant in their refusal to tell Angela, and because his concern was to take care of the girl, he proceeded—only for the time being, he hoped—on their terms. She suffered no ill effects from the second bone-marrow extraction, which confirmed the presence of the chromosome and the accuracy of the diagnosis of chronic myelogenous leukemia.

Leukemia, almost universally fatal in 1968, is an acute or chronic malignant disease characterized by unusual numbers or types of white blood cells in the blood, bone marrow, or other tissues of the body. The patient is likely to suffer from anemia, infection, and bleeding. Leukemia is classed as a form of cancer, and although it is a comparatively rare form, it remains—apart from accidents—the principal killer of children beyond infancy in the United States. Chronic leukemia is the more slowly progressing form, but chronic myelogenous leukemia usually converts into acute leukemia, resulting in death. The cause of leukemia has not been determined.

$\mathcal{A}$ngela did not die in six months. Week after week, as someone from the family stood guard in the waiting room, Dowling probed glands and nodes, palpated organs, took blood, and asked questions while her white count hovered between 11,000 and 12,000. Through a year of visits she asked no questions while continuing to suffer. Sometimes, in school, she would open her mouth to recite and blood would pour out. Between classes, she would play "vampire" with classmates, who would run from her in mock fear. But she couldn't run from her fear. She had never been a good athlete, but now she was terrible—too weak, too slow, too careful. Too much pain.

Home was sweet. She had always been close to her family but often frustrated by their strictness. Suddenly she gained ground: she was free to do some of the things she had never been allowed to do before—provided she was accompanied by a member of the family. This was real progress! But she was too tired to enroll for the textile-designing classes she had craved in an effort to please her sister, Camille, twelve years her senior, married, and still her best friend; too listless and uninterested to take the piano lessons she and her parents settled on after her desire to play the drums like her brother, Philip, had been quashed. Too uncomfortable to go to the movies with her father on Friday nights, as always. Unable to stay up afterward as he repeated for her mother and her their favorite story from his storyteller's repertoire, that of "St." Crescitelli, a remote relative whom he was so proud of, a Catholic missionary in

China who had performed two miracles, one short of eligibility for saintdom, when he was martyred in 1900, his head thrown into the ocean and his body buried in the sand, and who returned, walking across the water intact, for his third miracle. Unable to keep her eyes open. Too sick, too sad, too alone.

And suddenly her white cell count began to climb: from 12,000 to 20,000 to 30,000—50,000—over 100,000! At the hospital they began to fear that it was too late for her, that the angel had sailed right past them. With few choices of treatment available to him—she was so young a victim—Dowling prescribed a radical experimental program of radiation to the spleen, an eventual splenectomy, and chemotherapy. For Angela, the only explanation: there is something not right with your blood.

When I was asked to listen to this story, my first impulse was to cover my ears. By listening to it, I could, I might, catch it.

When I finally accepted an invitation to lunch—I put it off so long that I obligated myself—I expected we'd meet at some customary midtown restaurant, my territory; not, as she specified, near the hospital, hers. The answer to my tentative "How near?" almost precluded this book. I was promised "a cozy, quiet little spot called The Recovery Room."

Angela is lovely, petite but not delicate, and charming; from the moment our elbows hit the table, I can't take my eyes off her. Her eyes are large and deep and brown, almond-shaped above high, angular cheekbones, dominant beneath finely arched expressive brows. She has a straight, slightly upturned nose, hollowed cheeks, and full lips. A face that narrows evenly to the converging lines of a strong jaw. A wide smile that shows a lot of teeth. Long, slender neck, thin wrists, elongated hands and fingers. Short auburn hair and—as she leans back and settles into her chair—great legs. She doesn't remember ever being well, but she doesn't look as if she's ever been sick. She's all smiles and gusto as she tells me about it.

She can't supply the exact timetable of events—the hospital records will do that. No use going to her for details about operating-room procedures either. She recalls a scalpel as something she used to open lichee nuts with late at night. Chemotherapy is so potent that a young friend undergoing it swore to her that ducks were always biting his behind. She's not supposed to complain about pain anymore—after ten years she should be accustomed to it. When she finally had the last rites memorized, they revised them.

She wants her story to be written. I write to stay alive, to live a little longer than I can live life. She wants her story to be written for the same reasons. Very well, but how will anyone ever know which chapter of her life he's on, where the book begins and ends?

She wants it written so that some will know there is hope. And others will understand: she describes the prejudice that accompanies disease and seeks my concurrence in condemning a relative for having once *kept special, secretly marked dishes for her visits. She drops her napkin and I, for the first time in my life, am too slow to retrieve one.*

She asks, "Will you do it?" I think: I am the unlikeliest person in the world to write this book. Sickness—anyone's—sickens me; disease suffocates and makes my mind crawl. For death, there are no words. "Will you?" But this is life—insistent and irresistible. I know her pretty well by now; I gulp and suggest that she should get to know me a little better. "I don't have time to waste," she says. "Where I sit, you get used to making fast decisions. And the right ones."

"To look at me, you wouldn't know that I've been dead for ten years. I became two Angelas—the high school kid and the girl with the anesthetized knowledge of death. I had to force myself to be a teen-ager. Swollen glands made the Beatles sound different."

In high school she joined the drama workshop, where she felt she fit in the best. She made a quick assessment: other girls had beauty, great figures, sophistication—she had her cheekbones. She was encouraged by her aunts and uncles, who she thought were impressed by her talent. It never occurred to her that she was getting all that attention because she was dying.

Her girl cousins hated her. "They resented me, didn't know I was really sick, and made fun of everything I said and did—especially my dramatics. When

I didn't know the songs they sang—because I liked show music, and not rock-and-roll—they said, 'You don't know anything!' When I explained, they came closer to the truth than any of us realized: 'You're really sick!' " She became wary about showing her feelings for anything, for fear they would use it to hurt her. She was sure that was why her mother had forbidden her to mention her hospital visits to anyone, especially her cousins.

She was a very good dancer. She had to be—it was the only thing that made her a real teen-ager. But after the family had formed a circle around her and urged her on at several family gatherings, her cousins informed her that she was making a fool of herself and everyone was laughing at her. She stopped dancing. "They were girls and they were cruel. No man has ever deliberately inflicted so much pain on me. I have never completely trusted other women since then. To me, they are to be treated with great caution, just like so many cousins."

Her "cousins" in the drama group weren't any better. She was crazy to know what a man was like, what a kiss was like. But every time a boy went as far as to hold hands with her, someone else got interested and wound up with him, usually later the same day. She was the foreplay, or so she thought, and the other girls were the sex.

"There was one boy, and one of my cousins had fixed me up with him. Without my parents knowing, of course. We were over at her house on a Saturday afternoon. She had told me how to talk to him—to agree with everything he said. So he talked and I agreed. Then he went to kiss me and I wanted him to. But he wouldn't hold still. I didn't know how long to hold my breath, which way to tilt my head, where the noses were supposed to go. And he kept moving like he was drilling for oil. Then I noticed a large, framed photograph on the piano, and said, 'Oh, my God, my grandparents are watching!' I couldn't do anything after that. I lost him. After he left, I wanted to know how I kissed. So I kissed my thumb and forefinger. I concluded that I must kiss pretty well—it felt good."

For a long time Angela didn't tell anyone about having radiation treatments. Her mother had been so firm about her silence that Angela was embarrassed about them, even ashamed of herself. When she did mention it, as casually as possible, to a few friends in the workshop, they didn't believe her, because they were as ignorant of the implications as she was and because she was so "on" all the time. And because Angela, while on radiation, had gained ten pounds—mostly in her chest—since she craved spices, garlic, and salt, and couldn't eat enough macaroni to satisfy herself. She looked . . . healthy. If, in the throes of the bohemian theatre life, Jana was advocating free love, Ellen was toying with suicide, and Dorian was re-examining his sexuality, why shouldn't Angela be an expiring heroine?

"Every girl in the workshop had a crush on the director, Jerry Fishman, who had a large mouth and buck teeth and looked like a fish fountain—surrounded by thirty-four nymphs. I thought my sickness might be good for something—to get his attention, which I craved like macaroni. In the lunchroom, with only twenty girls around him, I said, 'Jerry, I'm on radiation.' He ignored me. Several days later, discovering him alone in the corridor after school, I pulled up to him and said, 'I'm going for my radiation treatment and I don't feel very well. Would you hold my books for me?' He refused. Either he was a bastard or he didn't believe me either. Either way, he was a bastard."

She began to miss classes, to miss more and more school. She felt like a liar and a misfit. She was unable to cope with school and radiation. She had red lines on her body that outlined her spleen. They didn't come off with soap. They were a constant reminder that she was different. At the hospital, they would take a picture of her, draw their red lines, take another picture, strap her down, close a steel door— with a sickening hollow thud—and watch her through a small glass window. Once, in the waiting room full of the usual middle-aged and old women, she was asked if she had had a mastectomy. She was startled—she hadn't finished adding yet and they were on subtraction. No, she said, no, not that. Honestly. Nothing like that. Then what are you here for? they wanted to know. Didn't anyone believe her? She didn't know; she was just getting radiated.

Soon the world at the hospital became more real to her than the one outside. She hurried there from school and never hurried home. She formed relationships she couldn't have outside. Professional people were dedicated people; so were sick people. She began to shed high school "friends" for friends who "knew where it was at." She preferred adults to teen-agers because teen things confused her. She preferred sick adults to healthy ones because she could take their illnesses—and hers—better than she could take anything else. It was becoming the only thing she knew how to do.

It took adversity to make her feel anything like normal. When something went against her, she thought, Look at the privilege I just got here! My mother yelled at me as though I were a normal person! Or, He hurt me—as if I were a normal person!

"He" was Ronald Ferris and he hurt her because she wasn't a normal person. Philip and Johanna, her sister-in-law, had fixed her up with him, which was all right with her parents as long as she was with Philip and Johanna. It didn't stop him from whispering in her ear, more than once, "My name's Ferris, let's go around together." It didn't stop anyone she mentioned his name to from asking if he was a big wheel. It didn't stop her from going out with him. The name of the hospital did that. There aren't many laughs in Memorial Sloan-Kettering. He had dropped her off or picked her up there several times. One evening she had to return for the night—Dowling's orders—and when Ferris delivered her to the entrance, he clasped her hand and informed her that his dad had died of cancer and that he couldn't see her anymore because he couldn't let himself get any further involved. And she thought: What's that have to do with me? But she accepted his explanation because it made it that much easier for her to withdraw further into the hospital. Going round and round made her tired.

*M*onroe D. Dowling, Jr., M.D. Mad Dog coming and going. Someone had once called him that, but he wasn't mad.

He had a young daughter of his own. He had—had had—other young patients, many of them. His experience with teen-agers convinced him that they needed to be told quickly. He had seen too many renounce their families and disappear when they discovered no one had been "honest" with them. But the Ambrosias made the rules, different rules, and he had to play by them. He didn't want to lose her as a patient—that might mean the loss of a life. Not only would they take her to another doctor if he refused, they threatened to sue if he defied their decision not to tell Angela. He hoped that by gaining the confidence of the family he might be able to change their minds. He didn't want to lose her; he didn't want them to lose her, either; there was no telling what she might do if she found out.

She was willful and erratic. Her body was maturing rapidly; she was wildly immature. He gained her confidence with that first bone-marrow extraction—swift and painless. He acquired more: her admiration, her gratitude, her untested, undeveloped feelings. Her parents stood firm. She flirted outrageously with the doctor, who recognized that she was flirting with sex, flirting with life, and—if he failed to get through to her in some significant way—flirting with death. He had to make certain that she take the situation seriously without discovering the seriousness of it. He encouraged her—a little flirting of his own. She was encouraged. Her infirmity became a game she looked forward to playing. She used it to become a woman. To evolve. And Dowling, a man, enjoyed watching the woman in her evolve.

She was learning how to play, then using all the things she was learning to see what they would do to Dr. Dowling. And all the while he was learning from her. Finding out how she was functioning. Determining what to do over the next week or two. She'd tease; he'd laugh. She'd complain about nausea; he'd give her hell about her make-up. A veteran catcher—trying to keep the pitches mixed, humoring a nervous youngster shaking off a sign here and there and throwing what she wanted—he usually knew what they were going to do before they got there. It had to be that way to advance her medical program. Time up, usually extra innings, the conquering heroine would saunter—or sweep—out of his office, break stride as she reached the waiting room, and, girl again, go home with the chaperone of the day.

She never asked what was wrong with her. But after her visits, Dowling could always expect three phone calls. Mrs. Ambrosia would ask how her daughter was doing, perhaps a few more questions until she was satisfied that Angela was going to be all right for another week. Then big sister Camille would call, and in a sense, in the way she asked the questions and Dowling answered them, she was the patient, the one to be informed, to understand what was wrong and what had to be corrected and what was being done about it. She was the one Dowling tried to tell everything to, because she was the one, he knew, who was going to interpret the facts for the family.

Then came Camille's husband, Tony, to pick up anything that was too technical for Camille to fathom. So he could interpret it for her. So she could reinterpret it for them.

That was the family trio. Papa Ambrosia never called, but if something didn't go the way it was supposed to, when trouble occurred, he appeared. And, at home or at the hospital, when he put his foot down, everybody moved. He'd sit back and listen without comment, and then he'd ask two or three questions. Not technical questions. Not even important questions. Except that they were always worded in a way that made it clear he was going to be sure that nobody was careless, nobody was going to do something that could hurt a member of his family.

People share their illness. Particularly at Memorial. When someone develops leukemia, he or she joins an exclusive society which demands that its members converse with each other honestly and intelligently. In order to prevent interaction, Dowling saw her during his private office hours instead of at the clinic. At the end of the day.

Just when he was thinking he could think or feel no more that day, in would walk this refreshing young creature who enjoyed being gorgeous. Increasingly dressed to kill, to capture.

Or be captured. "I would do anything he asked. Once, trying to be discreet, he asked if I had any interest in pills for birth control. I asked, 'Do I need them?' He asked, 'Do you?' Being that nothing—

17

absolutely nothing!—was going on in my life, I didn't understand why he wanted me to have them. But if he wanted me to take them, I would take them! Then I thought: Aha, he wants to fool around! I got him now, I got him now! And no sooner did I think that than I chickened out, I chickened out!"

For the next twenty minutes or so, she was on the inside, "they" were just outside, and he sat back where he was, hands behind his head, and watched her perform.

"Angela, we physicians feel that when a patient isn't exactly up to par ... uh, we should get further into it and find out exactly what is going on; and, uh, I, as a physician ... "

Perhaps everyone had a "we physicians" speech coming somewhere in a lifetime, but why was hers coming so early? Dowling stammered and sweated and talked in circles until she finally picked out the word "operation." That was it, she had to have an operation!

"Yes, we think ... " And he started stammering again. She had imagined him—God, how she had imagined him!—but never had she imagined him like this: Mr. Cool wasn't so c-c-cool right now; in fact, he needed her help. He was adorable!

It was her scene to play. All she had to be was brave. Her mind shuffled from Katharine Hepburn to Bette Davis and back again to Hepburn.

"All right, I have to have an operation. I've already had my appendix out. What kind?"

Her Hepburn worked.

"A splenectomy."

"A what?"

"We want to remove your spleen."

She didn't know what her spleen was for. Or anybody else's. She began to weaken. Her Katharine Hepburn was abandoned, her Bette Davis forgotten.

"Does it hurt?"

"We have a wonderful doctor to do the operation."

There was her answer. He continued: "As part of the protocol we've put you on, we have to remove your spleen. We need your permission."

"Is it infected?"

"No, there's no evidence that it is. We can't really tell until we take it out. But it has become enlarged."

Of course it's become enlarged, she thought; they've been drawing red lines around it and radiating the hell out of it! It's their fault! But she was too frightened to say anything like that. They might get even.

"Do I have to?"

It was going to take some convincing. He knew, everyone knew, how much she wanted to have a child someday. She had bored her handful of dates with it. She ate up his and other doctors' hours with it. She broke her family's hearts with it. Dowling used it. To persuade her to have the operation.

"It could endanger a normal childbirth."

In plain words, she was conned. She agreed immediately.

Dowling didn't deceive her about the doctor who handled the splenectomy—he was wonderful to her. She still didn't understand why Dowling couldn't perform the operation himself but Dr. Lemuel Bowdin—a name she liked to drawl in a Southern accent—did everything he could to make her comfortable, starting by telling her what a pleasure it was going to be to operate on someone with such a good figure and then explaining that he usually had to cut through fifteen pounds of blubber. It was the word "blubber" that did it for her.

She was heavily tranquilized for the operation, but not so out of it that she didn't miss Dowling. "I was sure there was something he could do. After all, he *was* a doctor. I felt abandoned, and refused to let them start without him. Being told that he was on vacation made me feel worse. But Bowdin assured me that 'he's here in spirit.' I guessed that was better than nothing, and with that they proceeded."

She woke up with tubes coming out of everywhere. "Even my nose! I was an old hand at vomiting, but this hurt. They gave me codeine to stop that pain, but codeine makes me vomit. The pain across my stomach was unbearable." Demerol for that. For a week, nothing could reach the pain. She was surrounded by visitors who brought flowers she couldn't smell and candy that they ate. Every time someone touched the bed, she went up a wall. No one visits someone in the hospital without at some time touching the bed, and after she confirmed this she begged her mother and Camille for no more visitors.

"I spent a week on my back, without ever moving,

I think, and just as I was ready to get off it, I began to develop fluid in my lungs. From not moving. A nurse would push down on my stomach, which would make me cough, and up came the fluid. Otherwise, there was the danger of pneumonia. Through what I attribute only to negligence on the part of my body, I somehow managed to miss this one."

Bowdin took her for her first walk down the corridor. Bag and baggage, she was quite a sight. All her tubes, the ones leading out of her, and the ones leading into her, were grouped together into two "suitcases," which she had to carry. "Forever after, when someone says, 'You're full of it,' I will become self-conscious that the wrong tube was, and still is, connected to me."

She started to become her old self again, or, as Bowdin put it, unmanageable. When he came to remove her stitches, a combination of fear and modesty inspired her to draw the curtain surrounding the bed, excluding only her head, which remained outside so her eyes wouldn't have to observe what was going on. It wasn't till the eightieth stitch that she finally stopped counting and agreed to join him.

"For the removal of my tubes, I had him at an even greater disadvantage. When he started the final drainage siphon of the tube between my ribs by drawing air through the open end of the tube with his mouth, I sucked in my cheeks, opened my eyes wide, and started to rise upright. It's no wonder he didn't believe me at first when I refused to take a bath because I was sure that my insides would fall out."

Bowdin was proud of operation and patient and

21

retreated from her life stating that he was sorry he hadn't signed her stomach right next to the best—for him!—of all possible scars. Dowling bounced into her room and, as happy as she was to see him, she couldn't restrain herself from ordering him to "get the hell out."

The spleen, by the way, was healthy.

She was handled day and night. She had been cut and sewn; strapped and clamped—was swabbed, scrubbed, shaved, and sponged; stuck; "scoped"; dressed and bandaged. But no one *touched* her. Her only connection to the world outside of herself was one big surgical finger.

She collected a few issues of *Playboy* and *Vogue* from the waiting rooms and read them at night. "I wasn't a Bunny, but I still liked what I saw when I looked at myself in a mirror. I had a good figure." What it was good for was still part of the mystery. She knew doctors liked what they saw. She had got used to that already and liked the attention. It made her feel sexy while at the same time she could claim total innocence. She knew she had good legs, the value of which her brother Philip had once explained to her: "It's not legs themselves, but what they lead to." Right now, they led nowhere. "I had large brown eyes, high cheekbones, a small, straight nose, and a mouth that my back issues of *Playboy* taught me was sensuous.

"I was curious as hell. There were mysteries,

things that frightened me. But I was never close enough to anything or anyone to get frightened. I didn't know what anything felt like. I wanted to be held.

"I was short, but so was Natalie Wood. I always wore make-up so I wouldn't look like I was dying. And I still had my hair."

She used to look in the mirror and wonder what it would be like if she didn't have any scars on her stomach. "I spent a fortune trying different cosmetics to make my scars lighter. The real reason I got *Playboy* was to see a normal stomach. I could stare at a picture of one, or the real thing, if it presented itself, for an hour. Still, I was lucky. I looked good in negligees, and whatever I had that I couldn't get rid of, I could hide."

She had yet to have her chance to be a girl, but she was accepted as a woman among the other women in the hospital, every one of whom was older than she was and dying. Knowing life would never be the same for them again, they lived by talking it, particularly the sex part of it. It was all very intimate and beyond her, and all she learned at the time was that unfulfilled women were raunchier than *Playboy*.

"I wanted romance. My father had been very strict, but he had never forbidden romance. He hadn't even found it necessary to mention it. I figured if you got romance, sex somehow came with it and took care of itself. And that made sex, whatever it was when it came home to roost, all right. Once again, I had my state of innocence. But what took care of romance?" She thought she found the answer when she invented Dowling. But sex never came with it.

Not that she was sure she wanted it to. "It was something that could kill my father—that I understood, although I couldn't see how. Nor could I understand why most of the girls in the drama club hadn't lost theirs . . . their *fathers*. But I knew that I wasn't even supposed to be thinking about it, so when I thought about it, I felt awful and tried not to think about it, but that was always when I could think of nothing else but. So I thought about it and put together a crooked picture based on 'hand-me-downs' . . . and watched my father carefully for signs of deterioration."

Dowling was the only man in her life, but occasionally someone from school would show interest. There was one, a student teacher, who was interested enough to return several times, and in gratitude she ate the food he brought, read the magazines, and put the flower in a vase by itself. Dowling was never around when he visited, but she made him smell the flower and gave him an earful. "Chuck was tall and very handsome, but I made Chuck even taller for Dowling and Dowling taller for Chuck. Both became taller and handsomer and I believed every lie of it."

While other girls her age spent endless hours in front of their bathroom mirrors primping for dates, Angela fussed and worried about the neatness of the tubes coming out of her arms. A visitor had once walked in while a nurse was repairing an intravenous tube that had come loose. No such thing was going to happen with Chuck. She was in a wheelchair at the opposite end of the corridor when Camille, who was taking her for a walk, spotted him.

"Chuck who?" and before Camille could say, "Your Chuck," Angela repeated his name and said, "Get me out of here!" She slid down, Camille swung around, and, picking up speed, they retreated.

"You can't do this. What if he sees us?"

"He's not going to see me like this."

"But where are we going to go?"

"I don't care. He's not going to see me like this."

She thought she knew every hiding place on the eighth floor, but she found a new one. It was four by eight and smelled of starched white linen. And had no air.

"We can't stay here."

"Just until he leaves."

"Angela, that boy isn't leaving. He knows you can't be very far away."

He had only seen her at her best. She didn't care if she never saw him again, she didn't want him to see her "like this."

They each helped themselves to a towel.

"Look, you're going to get pneumonia. I've got to get you out of here."

Angela started to cry.

"Ange ... "

But there was nothing Camille could say. Angela didn't want him to see her in a wheelchair. She listened to an interior voice: There she is ... cage three.... We have the species of the dying breed—

the poor girl trying to hang on to life. Let's all have a big round of applause and feel sorry for the poor creature in cage three. . . . "I didn't know I was really dying, of course, so I wanted to die. I told Camille that."

Camille got angry, then hurt. "All right, I'll get him out of there. You have twenty minutes."

While Camille tugged the bewildered innocent by the hand and led him in any direction but her sister's, Angela had twenty minutes to wheel herself back to her room, get back in bed (by herself), change her nightgown (herself), and put on fresh make-up. And a fresh, nothing-out-of-the-ordinary smile. "But when he entered, the room became something else and I was no longer a hospital patient. He was beautiful." It was his last visit. She never saw him again.

But soon she began to have a lot of visitors—at night, in her head. Some very special ones. Not only Dowling, but several other doctors from the hospital. Several boys from school who had never even looked at her before. And then, right after she had seen him on *Medical Center*, Chad Everett. And more.

"I wanted so much to be held that I'd begun to put a pillow down right next to me, and I would lie on my side right up against it, facing it, and make believe it was the 'he' of the day, or the week."

No matter what kind of room she was in, ward, semiprivate, or private, she always closed the curtains around her bed. Completely. There was a little bit of touching herself, but touching in a hospital is limited. For the most part, she just tapped her imagination.

She would see someone that day and think: That's who I want to be with tonight! He always showed up—on time. Sometimes in the evenings she would shut people off—sometimes abruptly—so that she could be with her pillow-person sooner.

"My love and I were alone. We would whisper. I heard both my voice and his voice, his exact voice, in my head. In the dark I saw every gesture, every detail of his features. He would often answer questions for me that no one else could answer. Together, I thought, we might even solve one of my 'impossible' problems.

"My man of the night never rushed me. He was always gentle, and always understanding. And never, ever, tried to go too far. We slept in each other's arms."

They were on a yacht. Or in a bed on an airplane. Or camping outside while it was raining—completely covered by sheets.

"He was all mine. I was his. But I always kept the upper hand. He was lucky to have me."

If her nights were so crystal clear, imagine the unreality that clouded her days.

The same girl who could embrace so many men by night was thrown into a panic on being informed that she had to have what would be her first internal. Not only was it a question of modesty, but one of fear. "I knew the bottom of my stomach had pain and I didn't want anyone touching it from the inside. I figured you're closer to everything on the inside. Right?

Dowling tried to tie this one to having a child some-day, and it made sense, but on principle—remembering my spleen—I wasn't buying. Camille took a different tack. She said it was terrific, that I should close my eyes and enjoy it—'You'll probably fall in love with the doctor that examines you'—and added in a hushed voice that Dad would never know the difference. She didn't convince me, but she swayed me a little. Dowling and Camille. Camille and Dowling. As a last stand, I warned both of them: 'If this guy has long fingers, I don't want any part of him.'

"The doctor who turned up had long eyelashes. And long limbs. He was long on charm and good looks and seemed short on nothing. He was black and beautiful and, as he entered the room, he introduced himself by saying, 'I'm going to give you an internal.' I said, 'You're going to give me shit! You're not coming near me!' "

She didn't look at him once during the examination. "But I said something terrible about my sister—just before my eyes crossed and the pain put me away."

"Excuse me, God, I know this is no place to talk to you from ... "

She was hiding from treatment. In the eighth-floor ladies' room.

" ... but it's the only place where I can be alone."

She was in the third stage of the protocol: chemotherapy. Deliberately aggressive chemotherapy. As Dowling and the nurses paraded around the intravenous pole, she heard words like "Ara-C," "thioguanine," "L-Asparaginase." No matter what it was called, it made her indescribably sick. What Angela didn't know was that she was the subject of an experiment, the guest of a government grant. She was serving as a guinea pig for L-Asparaginase, the new, untested drug. She was watched constantly.

"I'm not asking you to make me well. Only for the strength to see it through so that I can make myself well."

Her faith was unshakable. She and her father were the devout Catholics in the family, the twosome at Mass every Sunday. Once, when she was ten, he had been too sick to go; in desperation, she sneaked out of the house carrying her communion Bible and went by herself. When she got home, her father gave her hell: the only thing worse than a good Catholic girl not going to Mass was a good Catholic girl going anywhere, even to Mass, by herself.

"Bless my mother and father, Camille and Tony, Philip and Johanna. And Dr. Dowling. Amen."

Camille found her in the ladies' room, where Dowling had suggested she look, and brought her back.

She was watched constantly, by her family as well as the staff. They never left her alone. They were there at 8 a.m. and they were there for the day. For dinner and until they were asked to leave at night. The hospital was alive with dangers to her innocence: there were interns and there were patients.

A hot-to-trot intern would overenthusiastically

pop in on a morning to play. But Mother was there and sister was there, and in spite of whatever encouragement he had been given the night before, nothing was going to happen. She had been playing games, too.

When she was feeling well enough to be interested in other patients, they were never able to get near her long enough to exchange more than casual greetings. The most she could learn was a few Christian names. If they looked leukemic to Mrs. Ambrosia, it didn't even get that far. Mama—all of them, at her orders—was on hand to make sure of that.

For the most part, Angela was too sick to be interested in patients or interns. She was weak and nauseated and vomiting constantly. She had a fever, a dry cough, occasional bleeding under her skin, and some blood in her urine. The family did all they could think of to do for her. Aunts and uncles brought stuffed animals and homemade cannoli. Camille and Tony bought endless ounces of perfume and make-up—and nightgowns. Her brother Philip and his wife, Johanna, hung a menagerie of tiny dolls, charms, and vines from her i.v. pole. Her mother wiped her brow every five minutes and presented her with a four-dollar deluxe turkey sandwich on an Italian roll every single night—even if Angela only took three or four bites! Her father brought more stuffed animals, and sang for her in the beautiful bass voice she loved so much. She didn't ask any questions. She didn't need to know.

*D*uring the day, she told the time by her medication—every four hours. Nights, however, were endless without the four-hour intervals. As soon as the night nurse had finally cleared the room of visitors, she would bring Angela a paper cup containing a handful of tranquilizers, sleeping pills, and pain-killers, which were supposed to hold her for the night, along with a mouthful of comforting words—"Here, sweetheart, I hope the pills are working for the little girl!" Angela began to recognize the various shapes and colors of the pills, and to count them as if she were making sure that they were all there. Twice she found a few new ones and questioned the on-duty nurse about them. "Just take 'em" was the answer she got, with the explanation "I've got a lot of work to do. If I stopped and answered questions for every patient . . . " On each occasion, she refused to take the pills, any of them, until the nurse at least agreed to return to her station and check Angela's chart. Both times the nurse returned silently, sullenly, with none but the customary pills. But the next time Angela was in pain and wanted her pills a few minutes early, she was perfunctorily told that her chart said bedtime—9 p.m.—and she would have to wait until the exact time.

She had been confined in the hospital long enough to learn that you bargain for everything. She did her best bargaining at night. It took her all day to get those starched sheets broken in; then they wanted to replace them. But if the nurse would let her keep them till the next morning, she promised she would go right to sleep. That was the kind of deal nurses liked. One night nurse was sensitive to the sight of blood and other body fluids. Angela offered to sponge-bathe and clean herself if the nurse would help her out of bed, prop her up in front of the sink in her room with the back of a chair, put out the lights, and leave the room, closing the door behind her. Angela would ring for her when she was ready for bed. Totally nude, a flashlight held between chin and chest—the way the nurses did to free their hands when they took her pulse in the dark during the night—Angela would dip a towel into a sinkful of piping-hot water, wring out the towel, and—after she had washed herself—lay it on each arm, her back, her chest, her stomach, her hips and buttocks, each leg, replenishing the towel with fresh hot water between applications. She was always chilled and the heat felt good.

One night she had the feeling that someone was watching. The door wasn't completely closed and, through the crack between the door hinges, someone *was* watching—a young male. As she tried to cover herself with the towel, she asked him how long he had been there, but he wouldn't answer, wouldn't say anything, just stood there. She tried to block his line of sight, tried to cover herself again, but it was no use; no matter what she did, she still felt exposed and naked. She dipped the towel into the hot water, swung the door open, and threw it against his face. He screamed, she screamed, and the nurses came running as lights went on all around them. While one of the nurses dressed her quickly and another led the boy back to his room, still another nurse scolded Angela for not being in her bed, where she belonged.

Sometimes nights were filled with "stomach-turning sounds and smells." People in pain scream, "Mama, Mama!" The patient who feels no pain that night feels guilty. Sometimes Angela tried to use her imagination to twist her senses, to drown out the cries and the crying, the sirens and the machines, with a ship's foghorn, the engine of a passing airplane, rain against the windowpanes. Because she was still frightened of being away from her own mother, she tried to imagine that she could hear, muffled by distance, her mother's voice—"the two-by-four with the six-by-eight mouth," her relatives called her—doing all the talking and making her husband feel as though he were making all the decisions (a tactic she had once admitted to Angela). To cope with the odors, to block out the burning in her nostrils from alcohol, surgical scrub, and antiseptic, Angela would think of her mother waiting for her in front of the house as she always did in fair weather, and smell spring and autumn. Or see her on the stairway polishing the banister, and she would smell lemon. Or picture her father and mother in the kitchen together—she stirring and scurrying and hurriedly swinging the oven door open; and he painstakingly arranging his wife's delicate pastries on a serving tray—as the aroma of fresh baking floated through every room of the house.

It always seemed that she had just fallen asleep

when several nurses would come in, around 4 a.m., to fill her pitcher with ice water. With ice cubes, clattering, pounding ice cubes—and talk about the latest sale at Macy's, in full voice, because nurses never whisper.

Every once in a while, one of the nurses would ask her, in the middle of the night, if she would like something to eat, but that was all right; that was like home.

Mornings, which often began as early as 6 a.m., were humiliating. She was horrified by the volume of traffic, male traffic, in her room, coming as it did at the worst moments. There was always the sponge bath—always too cold!—that made her nipples hard, and she couldn't bargain her way out of it the way she did at night. There was always the bedpan—sometimes an enema *plus* the bedpan. Sometimes an intern *plus* enema *plus* bedpan! No matter how much she succeeded in making a good impression on hospital personnel—and she tried—there was always that bedpan. Dr. Dowling entered her room one morning while she was on the pan and either didn't know that she was or pretended not to know. As the sides of the pan dug into her, her sides grew so sore that she finally had to ask him to leave her room for a few minutes—she wasn't moving until . . .

They asked for a urine specimen. She didn't have to urinate. She was told she had to. She said she couldn't. They said she could. She said she couldn't, not with six people around her. She asked permission to go into the bathroom "like a dignified human being." They said she couldn't go by herself, she might pass out. She agreed to a nurse accompanying her. As she sat on the toilet, her legs spread, the specimen jar between them, the nurse crouched, looked underneath her, and asked if anything was happening. Plenty was happening—inside of her—but Angela couldn't seem to make anyone understand that nothing productive was going to happen if they continued to hover and stare. Instead, they tried to *make* things happen by pouring warm water between her legs.

She fought back against the dehumanization. As soon as the morning's ministrations were completed, she would slip away from her room, moving slowly, toting her i.v. pole with her, to a little alcove with a wide wall grating open to the outside, and, with a sun visor that she had got Tony to buy for her, she would sun herself. For the next half-hour, until her mother was due to arrive, she was "at the club." Afternoons, she would get permission from the nurse on duty for Camille to help her with her bath, excuse herself from the rest of her family, and she and Camille would adjourn to the bathroom for her Phisohex bath—concealing a split of champagne, two goblets, and a candle. She fought the unpleasantness of the hospital the way she fought the rigidity of home, the way she fought the loneliness anywhere—with style, with fantasy. No matter where she was, she was always fighting to get out of her environment.

*T*he home she returned to when she was allowed to return home wasn't the same home she had left behind. Her role was different, even though no one admitted it. Every confirmation of the change made her die inside a little bit more. The Ambrosias had always been a very open family. Papa Ambrosia insisted on it, and that was all that was necessary. Although Angela was six years younger than her married brother and twelve years younger than her married sister, any family session of consequence that included mother, father, Camille, and Philip included her. Suddenly there were whispers and discussions that always seemed to end just as she entered the room.

People whisper around sick people—the hospital had certainly accustomed her to that—so for a while she shrugged off the hushed voices. Then she began to notice that they actually raised their voices when they first confronted her. Sometimes they seemed startled by her. Had she been away so long that they had grown unused to having her around? The abrupt termination of intense family conversation and the awkward segue into the artificially bright "Hi, Ange"s that bombarded her and held her at arm's length while they gathered their composure and stuffed their discomfort under the living room's upholstered pillows made her wary, and self-conscious.

"It was as if I should wear a bell around my neck to warn the innocent of the approach of the unclean—the family leper. On the few occasions when I didn't feel they were frightened of me, I felt they were disappointed in me." But that hurt her so deeply that whenever possible she gave them fear as their out.

If her body was working overtime to produce white cells, her mind was no less active. "My imagination had already supplied a rich fantasy life, complete with drama: my ward, as viewed on a seventeen-inch screen; and romance—the patient's doctor, of course. Now there was intrigue—in the parlor! But I didn't imagine the whispers and the starts. I was right about everything. Everything that is, except Angela, alone, at the center of it all. Because right there in the center with me was my mother." Still trying desperately to protect her daughter, not only from the painful knowledge of what she had, but from what she, her mother, had. While Angela was in and out of the hospital, and during her first long stay, her mother had been diagnosed for breast cancer, treated daily with radiation, and somehow, between always being there to hold her daughter's hand and being home often enough to hold the rest of the family together, she had had a breast removed—without Angela's ever finding out. She healed especially fast because "my daughter needs me!"

"You look lovely, dear," her mother had once told her backstage after a performance of the school drama workshop, meanwhile deftly stuffing a folded Kleenex between her daughter's breasts to reduce the décolletage before Papa Ambrosia arrived. Mother had looked lovely, too. Angela had always

37

been so proud of her mother's youthful appearance, especially her compact figure; she and her sister were delighted when their mother was mistaken, in a dress shop or on the beach, for their third sister.

According to her medical chart, Mrs. Ambrosia's operation was a hundred percent successful. What the operating knife and doctors' reassurances had failed to remove was her guiltily harbored conviction that she was genetically responsible for her daughter's illness. Her overriding concern continued to be Angela. From the beginning, she had taken fanatic precautions against Angela's accidentally discovering anything about herself. She kept everything secret from friends and neighbors and, as long as she could, even family: Angela's own brother didn't know Angela had leukemia until he came across his mother sitting on a curb in front of a neighborhood shopping center, crying. It was this kind of secretiveness that first made Angela think that her mother was ashamed of her. Then, after her mother's own cancer diagnosis, there was the fear that if Angela found out what her mother had, she might figure out what *she* had. There was a lot to whisper about.

Soon Angela wanted to whisper, too. She wanted to ask her brother and sister what was going on, because she began to notice that her father was becoming less strict, and she could find no way to relate the change to herself. But, like everything else at that time, of course it did.

"My father was picking up the slack for my mother. In addition to putting in as much overtime steam-fitting as possible, so that he could pay all my mother's bills and the few outstanding ones of mine—and have something left over for a stuffed animal—he would help prepare dinner, clean up afterwards, and look for things that needed doing around the house. I remember him sewing—in his hands, it seemed like the most masculine thing in the world to do."

There was only one thing he had trouble handling, and that was the thought of so many strangers—from doctors to orderlies—handling his daughter. That made him tired . . . that and only that made him unsure of himself. After an unusually long and painful look at himself, he came to the conclusion, and then convinced his wife, that someone with a clearer head and freer schedule than either of them was able to have at that time had to be available around the clock for Angela. He didn't realize that this had happened already—Camille and Tony had become Angela's second mother and father.

Now she had three homes, and if the first two, her parents' and the hospital, were whisper-worlds, Camille's and Tony's was a shout. "Those two nuts" did everything they could to keep her laughing, which wasn't easy when she returned to their apartment after a day of chemotherapy for a night of throwing up thirty times or more. When Tony wasn't using his arms to carry Angela to the toilet she was too weak by this time to carry herself to, he was using them to break one pratfall after another. When

Camille wasn't holding Angela's forehead, she was holding her own sides as Angela held hers while they both urged Tony on to further heights, or falls. All night.

Mornings, Camille and Tony got up somehow and went to work, while Angela slept soundly, sometimes all day, on the couch in their living room, her bedroom. "It was there that the Angel of Death called on me. Disguised as my sister. I dreamed someone was knocking on the door. When I asked who it was, a woman's voice answered, 'It's Camille. . . . Open up . . . I have a bag full of apples.' I didn't believe it was Camille but I opened the door. She was wearing Camille's lavender outfit and pearls, and offered me an apple, but, thinking of Eve, I refused. She tried again and even offered to slice it for me, but I wasn't interested. 'Just take a bite,' she said, and I said, 'You're not my sister.' She shoved it into my mouth and forced me to, but I spit it out, scratched it out, as quickly as I could. That's when I was awakened by knocking on the door. I got up, shaking, and asked who was there. It was Camille—'Did I wake you?' 'Why didn't you use your key?' I yelled through the door. 'I have an armful of groceries. Hurry and open up . . . you want an apple?' Before I opened the door, I asked, 'Camille, are you wearing your lavender outfit?' 'Yeah, hurry up!' 'With your pearls?' 'Yes, how did you know? Open the door, will you!' And, sure enough, when I opened it, she was! And she said, 'Why is your mouth all scratched up?' "

From that day on, she began creeping into their

bedroom when she was sure they were asleep and curling up at the foot of their bed, like a puppy. And wouldn't have it any other way, try as they did to move a bed in for her. "No puppy ever had it so good.

"Certainly not mine. A few weeks later, when I was back in the hospital for more chemo, Camille and Tony gave me the cutest mutt, which they smuggled in with the help of a forlorn-looking resident, who immediately regretted it—because in my excitement, I unthinkingly proclaimed their visual similarity for all to see, and named mutt two, the dog, after mutt one, the doctor. Of course, I kept Thurman a big secret and tried to keep him with me in my room. But we really didn't have much of a chance." Not against the scourge of the eighth floor, Nurse Lysol Can. Relentless in her pursuit of germs, she lifted, between as little thumb and forefinger as she could manage, a hospital-corner sheet of Angela's bed to discover two perplexed coal-black eyes and a cold nose, and screamed her "greasy sludge, sticky valve" scream. It didn't create quite the hospital scandal she longed for, but she swore she would carry the image of her shocking discovery to the grave with her. "I hope so, because that day mistress and dog were instantly and violently parted, never to meet again. Except, perhaps, in Heaven. Soon after, somebody found out that even my puppy had cancer—on his back—and had to be put to sleep."

*A*ngela thought of dying—as an actress thinks of dying. She didn't think of death. The only good she could find in dying was to make Dowling cry. Then, until they met in another life, as she fully expected, both of them would know how much he really loved her. But the greatest good she found in living was living for him! Why make him cry when she could make him happy just by staying alive?

Dowling knew that her infatuation with him was going to be a problem. But right now it was treatment in itself. He would wake her by scratching her back every morning. She noticed that he always closed the curtain behind him. He would sit on the edge of her bed and talk with her. He always listened.

He told her, often, how beautiful she was. He meant it—it was there the day she came to him. But no one had ever spoken to her in those terms before. At seventeen, that was what she needed to know.

He could be counted on to make her feel whole in a dozen different ways. She had once winded him by re-enacting a Miss America contestant doing Lady Macbeth with a Brooklyn accent—"Owwt, owwt, daym spaht. ... Banquo is bayried. He *cayn't* come owwt from hiz grafe!" For a while he made her do it every time he saw her, and roared with laughter each time. He still asked for it; she did or didn't comply, sometimes blushed; it became their joke.

He had said that he wished all his patients were like her. She clung to that. At her worst moments— the vise-tightening under her arms, the ripping at the corners of her mouth, the toothache in her jaw and her joints, the ice picks in her distended

42

scar—she told herself: By being courageous I can make him run away with me someday!

Monroe Dowling wasn't falling in love with Angela. Dr. Dowling was already in love, as a doctor, with the life he hoped he was saving. He worked long, unusual hours—there was no certain schedule for saving unscheduled lives. In addition to morning rounds, he began to drop by at odd hours, any of the twenty-four. One 4 a.m., he appeared with a glow-in-the-dark Yo-Yo, which he could make "sleep" or "walk."

She wore make-up all day, every day. She began to put on fresh make-up before sleeptime and to keep it on all night. Sometimes she would manage to wake up extra early and make up all over again before he arrived. Beauty pretending to be sleeping.

This man, whom all the women in the area— doctors, nurses, patients—seemed to care for, cared for her. She wanted them to notice. She had just been refreshed—twice: sponge-bathed for the night by a nurse and perfumed and powdered by herself— when he surprised her. Had he stopped by to show himself off ? He was on his way to a roast-beef dinner and speaking engagement, and looked magnificent in his sharply cut, double-breasted dark blue suit. "How ya' doin'?," as usual. He closed the curtain and sat on the edge of the bed. He answered the easy questions. He grasped her hand and said he'd better leave before she and her fragrances intoxicated him and the dinner was left without its speaker. Power! As he started to stand, she pulled him down and hugged him tightly, quickly. He stood, smoothed out the sheet where he had been, and smiled. She hesitated, decided not to tell him that his suit jacket had baby powder all over the front of it. She wanted them to know that she had been hugged. He exited and she counted. She was on six when she heard the burst of nurses' laughter in the hall, in seventh heaven as it grew, louder and louder. She was afraid to laugh too hard, but she did. It was contagious.

She was sleeping lightly. She couldn't mess her hair; she couldn't smear her make-up. She thought she heard him and pretended to be sleeping. Someone with him? A woman? No, it wasn't Dowling; it was an intern. And a nurse. At the foot of her bed. He had his hands all over the nurse, who was stifling little noises, breathing hard. Was she dreaming? She could scarcely see them, but she could see the top of the nurse's whites disappearing. Please, Dowling—"How ya' doin'?"—now! More starched rustling. Laugh or cry? Giggle: she giggled and they scurried. She had giggled all right, but it disturbed her.

She had trouble sleeping every night now. Her mind was assaulted by sensation. Life was everywhere—it was even in the hospital. The pillow at her side was only a pillow, not a man. There was no pill, sleeping or otherwise, for that. Her body was getting large and uncomfortable. She couldn't lie still. Some of the night nurses would relieve the younger male patients when they bathed them. Nobody did anything for young girls.

Her mother wanted to know why she looked so pale, her eyes so dark and sunken, so tired. Dowling wanted to know why the nurses on the floor weren't looking after her more carefully. He had his part in control; technically, she was getting better every day now—her blood was the healthiest it had been! She heard him from her room: he was angry and he grew angrier with every proffered explanation.

She couldn't tell him. And she couldn't possibly tell him about the intern and the nurse. The curtain was closed. He sat on the edge of the bed. He was asking the questions. And she told him—she loved him. How deeply, how much, how she couldn't help herself. And wiped her eyes while he held her other hand. Then, a big girl, she asked him if he loved her and, like a big girl, she told him she didn't want him to give her a Marcus Welby happy-hour answer, and he didn't. He chose his words very carefully—this was surgery. He loved her, yes; she was very dear to him, more than just a patient; she had affected him very deeply—a doctor can't let every patient affect him that way. But he was a doctor, her doctor; he was a married man with two children. He was flattered, honored; he would always be, and they would be great friends always. But he had never permitted himself—he was not in love with her. And she told him she didn't believe him.

That night she slept. He didn't.

"Other girls my age sat in classes and signed their names Mrs. So-and-So in their notebooks to see what it would look like. I didn't have a boyfriend, but I had my Dowling! Other girls longed to get out of their houses and have their own apartments. I didn't

45

exactly have my own apartment, but I was sometimes living away from home—Memorial Hospital
was my East Side pad."

She had a headache and no one panicked. She
caught a cold and half the hospital staff didn't
come running to her bedside. She was sure that she
had finally pushed Dowling too far.

Dowling couldn't tell her how proud of her he was.
Her most recent tests determined that the Philadelphia chromosome was absent. Angela Ambrosia had
become the first person in medical history ever to
lose the chromosome, the first case where an attempt
was made to do it deliberately and succeeded. She
was a milestone. She might be in remission. Remission, in leukemia, means a pause or retreat by the
disease—no clinical symptoms, apparently normal
health with no certainty of permanence. There was
still reason for caution, but instead of being overcau-
tious with her—a cold! a headache!—a doctor had to
be cautious with himself. Dowling whispered for joy.

While she wondered why people were suddenly
relaxing their holds on her—again!—Dowling
avoided intimate contact with her, sent emissaries
from the laboratory, and tried to puzzle out what to
say. To tell her she was in remission was to tell her
what she had, and Dowling still had his orders. To
appeal to her parents was futile: Mama Ambrosia
had always—and still—refused to acknowledge that
her daughter was "that sick!"

The Ambrosias didn't feel the need to explain—they were simply taking her home. Dowling came shortly after eight that day—they were sure to be there—and with a solitary pat on the head and instructions to report to the outpatients' ward once a week for treatment, Angela was prepared for discharge from the hospital.

"I was thrown back into the world. I didn't understand what I had done, but I felt terrible about it. My body may have been better, but I felt sick inside. Sick and frightened and unwanted."

Still, she was going home. To her family, her house, her room. Dorothy returning safely from the Land of Oz. Her room—just as she had left it. But it felt different to her. She felt different in it. Larger or smaller, but definitely different, insisted Tiny Alice as she grew taller. "It's not different," said Papa Bear to Baby Bear. "It's not different," echoed Mama Bear.

You can deceive a young girl about what is in her body, but not about what is in her room. No one had been sleeping in her bed, but while she lay in the hospital, a burglar had broken into the house, ransacked every room, and taken just about everything that had a plug at the end of it. Her parents had tried to prepare things for her homecoming by replacing whatever was stolen, but the arm on the new stereo was a little heavier and the color of the new Magnavox a little faint. She felt betrayed. She loved them for all the trouble they had gone to for her, but these were mechanical things, not the stuffed animals that carried their love to her and gave her such warmth.

47

Everything was becoming a substitute for something else! Human contact, that was it. Rather than embrace her, they had reached out with a TV set, much as Dowling had buried himself behind his slides and extended a hand in a surgical glove.

She returned to school. But she was no longer a schoolgirl, and her classmates seemed trivial and idiotic. "Ambrosia?" "Present!" In body only. Present and accounted for: "Wow, we thought you were dead—do you see Denise anymore?" No one had sent even a flower.

She didn't see Denise anymore. Denise had graduated. So had Jana, she guessed. And what's-her-name. She didn't bother to remember.

Not even a flower! She hadn't thought of that before, why think of it now? Her courses were being taught in a remote language and her mind groped for a familiar word here and there. But math isn't taught with rads, and protocol is the way you conduct yourself in the cafeteria line.

Dead! She'd really get Dowling with this one. Twice as good as Lady Macbeth. A good thing they didn't send flowers, they'd probably be asking for their money back. That's how she'd end it—their money back.

This wasn't going to be as easy as she thought. She couldn't wait to be normal. She had to have it right away. Teachers were as impatient as she was; that much she remembered. She wanted to be reprimanded for not having the right answers. She missed a question and no one came running. And another. She had been an honor student, but missing felt better. It made her feel that she was fitting in. She kept it up; it reinforced her declining image of herself.

Finally, she got the kind of attention she thought she never wanted, but had become addicted to. In the isolation of the school principal's office, she accounted for her absence and described what she had been through. When she finished, the principal told her she had leukemia. Angela corrected her, explaining that it was a blood problem, but definitely not leukemia. The principal was adamant. Angela repeated what she knew, what she had been told. Mrs. Ambrosia was summoned to school, and flatly denied the principal's contention. Even with Angela absent from the room, Mrs. Ambrosia refused to admit that the principal could be right. Seeing no other proper explanation, no end in sight and, in view of her unacceptable classroom performance, no further reason for Angela to continue, the principal was forced to suggest that she leave school. Mrs. Ambrosia never wavered. She was willing to sacrifice her daughter's education to keep her from the truth.

Angela still had her blood tested once a week, and once a week she still passed the test. She would return to the hospital for examination and prescribed maintenance treatment at the "O.K. Corral," the fourth-floor outpatients' ward. There she would rejoin Alan and Russell, two young men who were on precisely the same protocol she was. Only—unknown to her—without her historic success. She had been written up in medical journals all over the world, but she knew nothing about it.

The boys knew; it gave them hope. She had made it, a little! Fortified by regard for her and forewarned by Dowling of the situation, they went along with the conspiracy to protect her. On the subject of disease, by any name, they were silent.

It was the first time Angela had ever had a chance to talk about "hospital things." For her it was sheer babble, gossip. They would sit and discuss their medication and how it was affecting them. They compared "battle scars" and exchanged home antidotes—salt for L-Asparaginase, beer and pretzels for methotrexate, BCNU, and everything else. In the same breath with which they shared their fear, they put on a brave front for each other. If the medicine worked for one, it might work for all. But if it *didn't* work for one . . . They feared not only for themselves but for each other. Good news was as impossible to share as bad: if one was doing particularly well, why weren't the others? In a transformation only they could understand, they became one.

Then, one day, Alan died—and part of Angela died with him. What was left to feel inside her felt, for the first time, like her own mortality. This wasn't *The Three Musketeers*—this could kill! Suddenly it was "Don't get too cute, Angela; don't get so damn confident, because he was—and he's dead."

The three had always telephoned to check on each other between hospital visits, but now Russell could no longer bear to call Angela; and Angela could no longer risk calling Russell for fear of discovering something she didn't want to know. A child puts her hands over her eyes and thinks that no one can see

50

her. Angela's version was to wear false eyelashes so the pain would not show.

She went to Dowling and complained that her right leg felt as if it were filling with hot liquid and was going to burst. He examined her, ran some tests, found nothing wrong, and told her to go home. She returned the next day in worse pain. He repeated that nothing was wrong, and with the pain traveling up her leg, into her lower back, and part of her stomach, she followed doctor's orders and went home.

She began to phone it in. His secretaries were like so many cousins, evasive and abusive, and when she did get through to him, he told her to try to relax. In order to get downstairs, she would sit on the top step and negotiate the flight downward with a series of slides and bumps. Slide-bump, slide-bump to the bottom, and then crawl. More calls and, pushed to the wall, Dowling prescribed wet heat. Hot towels in plastic bags, with two heating pads on top. And a visit to the hospital the next day.

Angela lifted her leg up on the examining table like a side of beef. "Take a look at this leg. The veins are out, I'm running a temperature, the leg is swollen, it is hot! There is something wrong with this leg!" She had just stated the textbook symptoms of phlebitis. The "side of beef" was the evidence.

She was admitted to Memorial. She was probed and pricked and scanned. Very late that night Dowling came to tell her that she had the ignominiously titled condition known as "milk leg." The leg swells and swells. And swells—unless something is done about it. She saw it coming and she wept. "You promised ... no more operations!" And before she could ask for time, he told her the truth. It was either operate or amputate. Operate immediately.

A doctor was flying in from California. While they waited ... more probing, pricking, and scanning. The internal. The tubes. The exploratory laparotomy. A thick needle jammed upward into the vein just above the inside anklebone. Dye, injected into the vein, to travel up the leg. She watched on "television"—they thought that would ease her mind a little—as it stopped just above the ankle. The show went off the air. Everything above the ankle was clotted.

More waiting. Blood transfusions. Please, God, no fiends or killers. Please ... no more tubes. She was drained.

Morning: Time to wake up and have her leg amputated, she thought.

The operation lasted sixteen hours. Technically: a thrombectomy, right femoral and saphenous vein; also excision of cyst on right fallopian tube. To her: scars, two on the surface and only one really visible—from her navel to her groin.

Right leg first, she stepped out of her unconsciousness. Even before she could get her eyes open, she slammed it against the protective railing of the bed. Unsure of what she felt, she slammed it a second and a third time—and more, without counting. A nurse, unable to restrain her, got a half-nelson on her mind long enough to persuade her to look. She opened her eyes; the nurse held the leg up high.

*D*uring her recovery, she met Annie, who was not so lucky. She had lost a leg to cancer of the bone. She had lost an arm on her opposite side. She had lost all her hair as a result of chemotherapy and a lung as a result of radiation. Finally, she had lost her parents, because they couldn't love such a loser.

When she didn't see Angela, as usual, by noon one day, Annie went looking for her. They were close in age and kindred in spirit; at a time when they were both having trouble "fitting in," they were perfect for each other.

Annie found Angela in her room, lying down. That was all it took for her to know that something was wrong.

Angela was convinced that her body could not take another operation. She had one secret, withheld even from her new friend: a pain in her lower back that had persisted for four days following the operation. She hadn't told anyone about it. Nor had anyone told her that following such an operation there were eight days between life or death—days haunted by the possibility of a blood clot breaking loose within the bloodstream and finding its way to the heart, the lungs, the brain.

Annie listened as Angela's halting speech got worse. "Don't you think you ought to tell the doctors?" They had already agreed on what frightened them most about operations: when they put you to sleep, you think you're never going to wake up again. Angela feared that the next sedative might shorten her life sooner than if she kept quiet and died "naturally." She was willing to settle for days.

"I can't. I'm scared." She started to say more, but she stopped breathing. She gasped for air and stopped.

Annie grabbed a vaporizer and shoved it in front of her. "Breathe!" She wheeled herself to the doorway and shouted Angela's bed and room number. "Emergency!" Bed and room number. Nurses appeared from every direction. Doctors, about twenty, circled like Indians around a covered wagon. Hands smothering, arrows striking front and rear, lungs burning . . . air.

Angela, barely conscious, remembers—when it came to death, these kids were professionals. Annie, bed and room number . . . Alan dead, and Russell— where? . . . Dowling, what took him so long!

All of three minutes. He took charge. Tubes in nose and arms. "Were you waiting for me to die?" Lung scan. Technicians fill in the corners of the room.

Mrs. Ambrosia arrived, an unexpected guest with a basket of artificial fruit. First a few tears of confusion, but then her confusion abruptly swerved, jumped the line, and, out of control, became hatred. What is this pulmonary embolism! What do you mean, a blood clot caught in the lung! This is my daughter!

The rest of the family had been summoned. Angela's eyes were closed when Camille entered. Angela knew her footsteps, knew she was there, was only building up the strength to frame and hold for a decent count. Camille wept, thought she was too late, prayed for a miracle. When Angela opened her eyes, Camille, after lying politely to the silence, turned and went quietly to the ladies' room, where all ninety-eight pounds of her seized a faucet and, in delayed hysteria, tore it out of the wall, plumbing and all. She was the next one to be treated that day.

The men arrived. Tony, Philip, her father. The patient knew what that meant. Her eyes trickled, her lips quivered. She broke. "Dad, please ... don't let them take me apart. I can't make it again. I'm going to die!"

Like the voice of God, he boomed, "You're not gonna die!"

There was no time to prep her, no time for another sweet needle. Barely time to remove a lung if that was necessary. She asked the priest giving last rites for a "double, extra-special whammy" and was wheeled from the living.

She had a blood clot and everybody had come running.

"**I** arrived by steel box. As I lay on my back watching the lights register and the floors flash by, I thought it might keep rising and transport me out of this world. But they were waiting for me when it stopped on the operating-room floor.

"The room was cold. They were laying out all the instruments that were going to be used, and it looked like ... utensils, like my mother's kitchen table before Thanksgiving dinner. And they were preparing me—and I felt like the turkey.

"It was time for the grand entrance of 'the frogs' ... the doctors, dressed all in green, and all you see is the eyes. You don't know what they're doing underneath those masks, so you look for the truth in the eyes.

"These eyes were smiling, but there were no wrinkles; the eyes were too tight, too plastic. And I knew this one was going to be a tough one.

"I didn't want the last thing I saw to be a tense face. Or a steel machine or a shiny instrument. I was looking for something to cross when the anesthesiologist entered. No one is supposed to wear jewelry in the operating room; she was wearing the largest gold cross I had ever seen. I looked and looked at it, and finally I asked if I could hold on. I clutched it as I started to go under.

"In school, I had cut the frogs open. Now the frogs were cutting me open.

"A frog asked, 'Is there anything you want to say before you go?' Go! I had been very quiet, because I didn't want to curse after I'd had my last rites. But where did he think I was going? 'Yeh. You guys screw this one up and I'll come back and haunt every one of you!' "

"I . . . couldn't see . . . the eyes. The frogs . . . were . . . carving . . . the turkey. The cross . . . my heart . . . the . . . frogs . . .

"Didn't get me! The first face I saw when I woke up was Dowling. Dr. Monroe D. Dowling, Jr., M.D. Smiling. I had made it! He was holding my favorite stuffed animal, Sam, in his arms, cradling it as he would a real cat, and petting it."

*H*er legs jumped. She laughed, and they jumped again. She waited . . . and they jumped and she laughed. She thought she had the damnedest act going—"Ambrosia and Her Jumping Legs."

She didn't feel any pain. She didn't feel anything but happy. Morphine-happy.

"They had promised me I wouldn't suffer for a minute. Otherwise I might have laughed till it hurt. After a few lost days in intensive care and a lot more in limbo, I felt so good it was frightening."

She was a floppy doll. There was an exercise chair—her "Frankenstein chair," she called it, because it went in all directions at once—that the nurses used to "pour" her into, which was good exercise for them, but didn't do anything for Angela . . . but make her laugh. "One of the nurses wasn't getting enough exercise, because she almost dropped me while they were putting me back to bed. It might have been the three incisions on my stomach, or it might have been my conviction that my insides were hollow—she let go and I folded in half like a soft

57

Milky Way. That was the end of the chair."

Every day for three weeks the doctors asked her how she felt, and every day for three weeks she giggled, and said, "Fine." Three weeks at 65 cc.s of morphine a day.

She wasn't surprised that someone had come in just to check her heart. Nor that he had awakened her in the middle of the night to do so. Nor was she displeased that he was very young and very handsome and a little self-conscious in her presence. "He had flaming red hair—I saw the top of his head a lot. With his stethoscope in one hand and then the other, and then the first one again, he looked and listened for my heart. Which was in my chest! Which was completely uncovered! After ten minutes, he said, 'I think we got a heartbeat here.' As much to relieve his embarrassment as to relieve mine, I put my head on his shoulder and said, 'Don't worry about it. At this point, I'm enjoying myself.' "

She slept well. When she told Dowling the next morning how sophisticated she'd been, he said—after he finished laughing—that it made him feel a little younger to know that the same tricks that worked when he was an intern still worked today. In the next breath, he said it was time to reduce her medication.

A few days at 55 cc.s, then 45 cc.s, and so on, until the end of the week, when those "jumping legs" were gone, along with the morphine. Her mouth felt like dirt and worms. "Ambrosia and Her Worms" wasn't so funny.

They asked her how she felt and she said, "Fine

... except my mouth." They said it was the after-effect of the morphine.

"But my legs began to get shorter." To feel shorter. She couldn't stretch them out far enough. She told herself it was the morphine. She still said "Fine" when they made their rounds: "My legs feel a little funny, but I feel fine."

She was afraid to complain. Since she had been "reinstated," she had been nothing but trouble. Their time was valuable. She wasn't doing what she was supposed to do. She was supposed to get well.

"They pointed out that I hadn't used my legs for almost a month, and I nodded and didn't say another word. In the hospital you learn how easy it is to make other people happy."

Her legs began to hurt. She had to sleep in a cramped position. She had to lie all day in a cramped position. She didn't have the morphine to blame any-more, so she persuaded herself that it was the clip they had put in her abdomen. That made the in-creasing pain more bearable. The clip was a sort of Mason-Dixon line they had inserted in her abdomen to prevent further clots from breaking off and scurry-ing directly north, like runaway slaves, to the heart or a lung. If it kept her body out of war with itself, she was for slavery.

When it was time to walk, she couldn't. They said she didn't want to. She suggested that it was the clip. They implied that it was her head. They convinced her that it wasn't the clip, but she failed to convince them of anything. She expected a therapist; they sent a psychologist. She prayed for help; her mother came and said, "They say it's my fault—I baby you too much. . . . Please, baby . . . " She pulled herself up by her intravenous pole to meet Dowling halfway; he held her chin like an orange, interrupted a tear with his forefinger, and promised her a gift the next time she walked to him. It wasn't a remedy but it was a deal.

"You don't *want* to walk" reverberated in her mind. A woman doctor, another "cousin" beneath the skin, goaded her with it. She slid down a little lower, braced for maximum support, and hurled, "Who the hell do you think you are to play God with me! You put your ass in this bed for one hour and go through the hell that I've gone through and let me see how you handle it!"

Dowling was brief about it: "You'll get your therapist tomorrow."

So that was what it took! "When do I get my present?"

"When you walk to me." He turned back to her in the doorway. "By the way, your lady doctor is a nun."

" . . . ! A wha . . . "

"God got ya'."

*A*nother handsome black, she mulled, only a little shorter—was it a policy of the hospital? She sat up a little and tried to look disengaged. Practically the first words out of his mouth were "I have some stockings for you." Too much! But it explained the tape measure running from the pink hip to the pale tip of her toe ... didn't it? "Let me show you how to put them on." She wondered how she would keep her father from killing him! But they weren't nylons and they weren't intended to complement her nightgowns. He produced a pair of Jobst surgical stockings, the ultimate Ace bandage, the ultimate in medical bondage. Designed to fit as a second skin, to increase pressure on the veins, to prevent the formation of blood clots by compelling circulation.

It was like forcing a two-hundred-pound woman into a size 5 girdle—they went on an inch at a time. Dresser and helper, in order to advance them, had to pinch and yank and, dripping with perspiration, stop for rest; then struggle again. On at last, the stockings did their own pinching—in the calves—cut behind the knees, and itched everywhere. Restricted everything. When they were removed—a few hours each day to let the legs breathe—the knees were usually skinned, the area behind bloodied. Then, wounds washed, legs baby-powdered or Vaselined, it was an inch at a time again.

He showed her once. It was the same with her exercises. Lie down, flat on back, bend this leg, then this leg, then both legs, to the chest, to the floor, to the sky, breathing in and out, if anything starts to hurt ... stop! This leg here and this leg here, legs together, push out with your heels, up with your toes, flex, point, down with your hands, raise your pelvis, lower, raise—not like that, not like that, like you're about to ...

Stopped. Palms down, pelvis midair, she looked at him blankly.

... You'll get the hang of it. If it hurts ... stop! Now, when you sleep, you must keep your legs absolutely straight—at all times; you'll want to curl up, but your muscles are contracting; you have to prevent that, so legs straight—no matter how much it hurts!

He left her with one final instruction, repeated more than once: "Don't overdo it." She did it most of the first night and the second—she'd show Dowling and her mother, she'd show everyone. Then she did it all night long.

That was when Mr. "Deeds" entered the case. He heard this grunting, this steady grunting. He was the head nurse on the floor, night shift, and that little girl had given him no trouble at all. He knew her chart, but he didn't know her; he was treated like a doctor at Memorial, and she'd never needed him. At least, neither of them knew she did until 4 a.m. that morning.

He didn't mean to startle her but he did. He was about six feet tall, very broad, very black, very dignified. Looked like Nat "King" Cole with a short Afro cut, a little gray at the temples. Honest eyes. Stern but humane. "And what surprise for Mr. Reeds have we here?"

Because she thought she was in *real* trouble this time, she attacked. "Who are you and what are you doing here? I'll give you five seconds to get out of here before I scream!"

"Give me five seconds to identify myself instead. I'm Mr. Reeds, in charge of this floor tonight. If you're going to scream, you might as well scream for me."

"Why did you sneak up on me like that?"

She needed him; he offered to help. When? If she couldn't wait, he couldn't either; why not right now? And they went to work, Reeds guiding her legs, counting, encouraging, forcing her to take breaks, guiding and encouraging again.

Even before she met him, Mrs. Ambrosia trusted him. The first line of Angela's description of Mr. "Deeds" reminded her of her husband: "He is as gentle as he is strong." He and Angela were working every night. Progress was slow, but they were a winning team, he said. He was never too busy. Or too tired—he began coming in during the day to show Mrs. Ambrosia what to do. She began returning to the hospital at 2 or 3 a.m., very soon simply staying there after visiting hours, working with him or in his place with Angela, always following his instructions to the letter, catching a few hours' sleep—between exercise sessions—on an improvised bed of coats, sheets, and pillow cushions at the end of the corridor. Soon both women were calling him Mr. Deeds, and he never corrected them. They thought it was the kindest name they had ever heard, and he looked forward to the affection he heard in the sound of it. When Angela finally discovered her mistake, he insisted that he was Mr. Deeds to her, and he could be no other.

"How we doin'?" he would ask every time he saw her. Before she saw him. He always sneaked up on her. And it was always "we."

She had worked harder than she'd ever worked before. Her gift was an oval mother-of-pearl mirror. As she made her way—a child learning to walk—to Dowling, he held it up to her. "I wanted you to see the smile on your face."

*S*he wants me to understand that this is a very private story and she'd rather not have it told.
"I'm telling you this because it's a beautiful story. And because you will know more about me from it. That's the only reason I'm telling you."
Just listen. Let her keep talking.
"If you can possibly change the story by not exactly stating things that happened and leaving it either to the imagination or handling it even more innocently in what had happened in a kiss or . . . in a touch . . . Or . . . we both went into the bathroom with the intention of fooling around, but I got scared and he let me out. . . ."
(Nervous laugh, voice rising.)
"Which is basically what happened!—but I mean before anything happened at all—I would really appreciate it. One, my family would not understand—I think you can understand that—I was eighteen—it's not water under the bridge. . . .

"My father could never, never, never forgive this, all right? Because I'm Daddy's little girl. So please, Ray, I'm ... "

(Nervous laugh again.)

"In walks one of the most beautiful experiences I've ever had in my life. A tall hippie by the name of Jeffrey Cruz. He had black eyes and light skin. Dark brown hair and an Afro which put a lot of people off—my mother and father, for instance. But he had great courage, which eventually won everybody over—even my mother and father, for instance. He had long, lean legs which were absolutely beautiful. And he had to lose one. He had bone cancer.

"Jeffrey would wait—we would both wait—for my family to leave every night. Then the evening would begin! He would come into my room and talk to me. Or read to me. Then we'd watch television together. After lights out, he'd plug his earphones into one side of the set and I'd plug mine into the other. What could be more natural for two people who were kept alive by being plugged into tubes and bottles day and night! He would push his chair close enough to my bed so that I could kind of cuddle in one of his arms and lean my head on his shoulder. I always felt safe with Jeff.

"I also felt special. He would give me every gift that he received. Or a flower from a bouquet. Or respect! Not that I'd ever lacked it from others. Before Jeff, I just never really knew what it was to have it . . . and know it . . . from a young man. He called me 'my lady' and even introduced me to his friends that way. Including a girl he had lived with. To me, he would say, 'This is my home now and you are my lady now.'

"I would give him some of my tranqs and pain-killers. Because he needed it more. When I thought it would make him feel better, I put on a dress for him.

"One night we were sitting at the end of the hall and I was wearing a peasant dress that Jeff loved on me. The nurse had just given us both our medication for the night and we were—basically, we were wrecked out of our heads; we felt no pain. And if we felt no pain, we felt fine. Jeff leaned over to me and said, 'Ange, would you meet me in the men's room if I asked you to meet me there?' (Both the men's and women's rooms were after-hours hiding places.) I said, 'No-o,' and he said, 'I knew it. I knew you wouldn't do it,' and I said, 'But I'll meet you in the ladies' room.' And he said, 'Really?' and I said, 'Yeh-uh, I'll meet you there-re.' And he said, 'Okay. You sure now?' And I said, 'Yeh-uh, I'm sure.'

"He went first. Then I went—through the hall-way with this out-of-control grin on my face. I entered the ladies' room—and he had shut the lights off, the little devil. Still supported by his crutches, he put his arms around me and sort of held on to the wall. And he kissed me—not a friendly kiss like all the ones before, but really kissed me! If I didn't know kisses went beyond the lips, I found out then, and I was fascinated by this new knowledge. And a little frightened. I'd never done anything like this before and I could tell you it was my conscience, but I think the truth is that I didn't want to mess up.

"He asked me to undo his robe and 'let his freedom go,' and I didn't know what he was talking about. He managed to make himself clear, and I became aware of this thing that had the strangest characteristics and was attached to him. What was this thing all about? I got really curious, so I asked him to put the light on, explaining, 'I've never seen anything like this before and I want to see what's doing.' He patted me on the head and switched the light on, and I . . . I started inspecting. I moved him left, I moved him right. I picked him up, I put him down. I got down and looked up, I got behind and looked through. I went everywhere fingers and eyes could go. What a work of art is man! It was actually attached! I looked again. I decided I liked the way he looked. He was adorable!

"He must have been suffering. So what if it was true that some of the saintly night nurses used to relieve the younger men when they bathed them! Jeff hadn't had a relationship with a girl in a long, long time, and here was this clown who was not only examining him and asking a lot of questions—hell, yes! I asked 'em—but I thought I was doing exactly what he wanted me to do! And pretty well! I guess one too many questions showed him the futility of the situation. He put his arms around me and kissed me again, but this was the old friendly kiss, and I started to cry just a little bit and I said, 'You're disappointed, aren't you?' And he said, 'No, not at all. You pleased me in a way I didn't expect to be pleased tonight.'

67

And I felt like a woman of the world.

"The next day I went out of my way to be pretty. Jeff kissed me on top of the head and told me how good he felt. Today, speaking as Mrs. Angela Rubel, I know he was a liar. A wonderful guy, but a liar."

"Whhen it came to death, these kids were professionals."

Corpses are removed by night. At first, the five or six, sometimes seven young people congregating in the corridor don't take much notice. Soon each in his or her own time begins to wonder what familiar face lies under the sheet. One night death is played out before them. "She was a young woman—I don't know anything else about her—and she was bleeding from all ends of the body. This was more than hearing or guessing. This was seeing. Jeff told me to stay with her while he went for Father Elder. She was well attended by staff, but we had our own things we might do.

"She couldn't speak, but she stared right at me, as I was to learn they all stare, as if to say, 'Please, please help me, please give me another few seconds of life.' I looked right back into her eyes, but there was nothing, nothing I could do."

Later that night Angela saw several drops of blood leading from that doorway. All the blood transfusions and surgical gauze pads in the world hadn't prepared her for the few spots of blood she had seen life reduced to.

"There had been many times, in great pain, when I wished that I could die. And times when I wished that I were dead. But when I got that close . . .

"I saw myself dying. I saw me bleeding and gasping. . . . "

She saw herself taking a little part of everyone with her and giving back nothing. She saw herself insensate. She saw herself without false eyelashes to hide the pain.

Life caught on among them like a fever—the children raged with it. They were children and happy to be. There was no limit to being young; they didn't know if they would ever be older.

It was a perfect Halloween night, in August. The rain raging outside had them huddled under an umbrella of their fantasies. The thunder brought out the macabre. In a corridor, in a corner, they exchange horror stories. Tonight's winner gets a prize. A death wagon drifts past. The head is carefully covered but the toe with the tag is not. Quick, a ghost story! Better, Angela requisitions a near-at-hand sheet, drapes it over herself, and stalks the toe. Bobs up and down. Becomes one ghost stalking another. Makes that haunting "Whoo!" sound that excited her so much when she was a child. Circles the wagon and swoops down, but not too close. Returns to the circle and takes a bow. If only Jeff had been here to see that. Or Annie. But Jeff had escaped the wagon, won his game already, been discharged. So, apparently, had Annie, who could leave the hospital on weekends now. Except, somebody noticed, this wasn't a weekend and where was Annie?

Annie's corpse was already out of the hospital by the time Angela learned that she had stalked it, haunted it, taken a large bow to large applause at the expense of her good friend. Cause of death: pulmonary embolism. Annie suffocated, died the way Angela almost died, the way Annie saved her from dying, only Angela hadn't been there to call bed and room number. Bed and room number. So much for children's games.

She turned to Dowling. She needed . . . something. He knew how much she was suffering, and hastily—recklessly, in light of the Ambrosias' imposed restrictions—prescribed a new "pet" of his.

She had been hearing more and more about Eric. Everybody was making a big fuss about him. While she roamed the corridors with her gang, it didn't matter. But if she had to share Dowling with him, she wasn't going to like him. . . . "No, thanks." She hated him. . . . "I'm sure he is." God, she was jealous. . . . "Some other time."

She clung more than ever to Dowling, who didn't have the time to stop and be clung to. The hospital had been her home and her sanctuary. He saw now that it might be her undoing. He prescribed a return to the world.

She was fitted with a heparin lock, a minute butterfly-shaped receptacle that fits into the vein just under the skin, with a rubber plug for the self-administration of injections of heparin, an anticoagulant. Every six hours, around the clock, no matter where she was or what she was engaged in, she was to give herself an injection.

To her, it meant freedom. To her mother, it meant total restraint. "It wasn't only life or death which stood in the balance; for me it was my life. I had never defied her wishes before, and I wasn't enough of a person to do it yet. But the only way I knew of to defy death was to prove life." She began to sneak out— just to do "normal" things.

Her cousin Joseph was the only young person her mother would trust with her. Cousin or not, Joseph was a man, and if the hospital had taught her anything besides how to give an injection to herself, it had taught her how to get a man to do what she wanted. "Joseph would have gone to the ends of the earth with me if he could have gotten me back home by dinnertime. An afternoon at the beach, my arm wrapped in a Baggie to protect the lock, was our proudest achievement."

*D*owling was on vacation and his stand-by unavailable. But it was a routine matter, the second or third time it had happened to her. A lock will frequently slip out of its proper position and can be replaced in minutes. Only this doctor was having trouble finding a vein. In either arm. Rather than admit incompetence, he switched her medicine. Coumadin didn't require a lock. It also didn't work for her, as her chart clearly stated. He ignored the chart and sent her home.

Two days later she was readmitted to the hospital. She had several clots in her leg and one small one in her lung.

She lay in bed trying to restrain herself from reciting her bed and room number over and over in her mind, as if she were memorizing lines, as if she were rehearsing her own death. She thought she heard Dowling's voice, but he wasn't due back until the next day, and when he didn't enter she dismissed it as wishful thinking. The next morning she learned that Dowling had been there in the middle of the night. *There*, but not here, she differentiated. Eric, but not me. She drew a deep breath and would have held it forever if her lungs had been strong enough.

When Dowling entered her room, she reached behind herself for Sam, that stuffed animal, the one Dowling had stroked, and hurled it at his head. Fluff by fluff in his direction, she cleared her bed.

Eric had been critically ill. Dowling had spent most of the night with him. He left it to Angela to find out for herself.

"It was strange . . . I had never seen Eric, but I could see him sick, and when I saw how sick he was, I felt awful."

Several days later they passed in the hall. They were both in wheelchairs, self-propelled. They recognized each other immediately and they both turned around. He was broader and blonder than she had imagined him and even in a chair he looked tall. His face couldn't contain his personality.

She asked him how he was feeling and told him

72

she was sorry that he had been so sick. He thanked her. It was the beginning of a wonderful friendship.

"We were both on the mend. We saw each other all the time—after visiting hours—but unlike Jeff, who always wanted us to be alone, Eric usually included us in the company of others. If we loved each other, it was in two very different, undefined ways. The only love we shared was our mutual love for Dowling."

Beyond Dowling, beyond Jeff, Eric had a way of blocking out the unpleasantness for her. She used to go out of her way to stand in his tall shadow. He would tilt his head forward and hug her with his long arms and she'd feel completely surrounded. She wouldn't have Memorial Sloan-Kettering et cetera around her; she'd have Eric.

She wanted to do the same for him. But when the chemo made him sick, he would ask her to turn her head. "He rejected my sympathy: 'What do you mean sorry? I'm the luckiest person in the world, because the medicine's working on me!' It took a long time for him to get used to using the emesis basin with me looking on. And when he finally let me hold it, or his head, it was as much of a shared intimacy as if he had disrobed in front of me."

When Eric spoke seriously, he sounded like a doctor to her. Most of the time she didn't know what he was talking about. He'd wait for a reaction, and when he didn't get one, he'd go on. But he'd always glance again at her with one of those parental "Is your nose running?" expressions.

He couldn't believe that no one had told her about marijuana for controlling the nausea from chemo. He even said that Dowling had a marijuana plant upstairs and was experimenting with it. "I told him it didn't matter anymore, because they hadn't given me chemo since the day I got the blood clots. He found that fascinating."

He tried to explain soccer to her, but she was always so caught up in the way he talked about it that she didn't pay attention to the game. "He loved to run with the wind hitting him in the face—I could see it, I could feel it on my face. I think that was what he missed most from life—his soccer games. He said that I should come up to his school for a soccer weekend someday, and I said I would, knowing full well that my parents would never let me go."

She learned from Eric, not from Dowling, that she didn't have to have another operation: "Being the one who gets to tell you is my gift for you—for getting well enough to walk in the world for me." She didn't know Eric meant that he couldn't follow.

"We were friends. We were in the men's room—just for privacy!—and Eric put his foot up on a latrine so he could see out of the high window. 'From high atop our beautiful East Side apartment.' He got excited because he spotted a bus, and he boosted me up to see it. Because—all because—it had color! Something other than white!"

"*I* was well. I asked my mother, 'Did I ever have leukemia?' She said, 'No. Never.' "

For four years, Angela believed every lie told to her. For four years, she cooperated by preserving her ignorance. Writers and weathermen draw conclusions. For four years, she connected all the dots and saw nothing.

Hospital psychologists explain a process of denial prevalent among terminal patients. Usually, denial is necessary for whatever day-to-day comfort a dying man can find. What is denied is death. Foremost, one's own; but the mortality of anyone with whom the patient identifies is a warning, a reminder, and an inevitable physical setback. The medical charts of an entire ward have been known to dip the day after one bed has been vacated. Consequently, not only is death not dwelt upon; it is, whenever possible, scarcely noted. Death is a failure of the patient, not the system. The system makes you well.

Before Angela had to come to terms with the prospect of death, her death, she had to face—or shy away from—its prospective cause. A healthy mind in an unhealthy body, she denied her disease. With an instinct that knowledge could be harmful to mind and body, she learned to overlook every clue. Even while she held the magnifying glass to others. Even when she followed the tracks and the paths crossed. For four years, for Angela, denial was practically synonymous with survival.

Did the others know? And know that she wasn't supposed to know? Eric had talked on and on about "leuk" one day, and not until she left his room did it

75

occur to her that she was playacting—pretending she was part of something that she wasn't part of and didn't know very much about. He had said: "It's not the 'leuk' that gets you, Ange, it's always something else." Why had he said that to her?

Every so often she would get a card addressed to the Memorial Sloan-Kettering Cancer Research Center. She once told Jeff how surprised she was to learn that—the "Cancer Research" part—and concluded it was that for some patients, but not for all. Obviously, she didn't have cancer.

She was well. For the few who get free from the "O.K. Corral" or get a reprieve from "death row," returning, even to visit, is too painful, too difficult. Just as Jeff, in spite of the best intentions, hadn't returned to see his "lady," she couldn't bring herself to visit Eric. Home again, from the outside, from the distance, she saw with unaccustomed clarity. Eric was seriously ill in a way that she had been seriously ill. No he wasn't. Denial.

Life became more precious. She was going to stay well. She was nineteen.

She slept late. She moved carefully. She kept her room very clean. She stayed home a lot ... in her room most of the time.

At first, her mother didn't know how to take it. Then the neighbors told her. It wasn't right for a young girl to lie around the house all the time. "This wasn't right and that wasn't right. So my mother scolded me, mostly in front of the neighbors, so that they wouldn't criticize—her."

Angela played volleyball in the backyard. With

an eight-year-old boy. Mama objected ... too strenu-
ous. Trying to please her, Angela joined her and her
friends in the sun on the front porch.

It was the first weeks in the hospital all over
again, with one sardonic twist. During those Valium
nights, long before she made any friends her own
age, she had been included in a society of old ladies
who clucked about the sex they weren't getting to
reaffirm the "life" they weren't getting. Here she
roosted, roasting. Listening to a neighbor, who'd
never been sick a day, peck on and on about the life
she wasn't getting—from her soapsuds, her vacuum
cleaner, and her relatives—to avoid facing the sex
she wasn't getting, or getting enough of, or was
avoiding. Or so Angela, simmering, conjectured.

"You look well," someone said. "The sun is good
for you." She was stifling.

She had waited until she was well to start feeling
sorry for herself. She knew how to use sickness, but
she didn't know how to use being well.

"I had never prayed to be healed, only to be normal. When it became clear that I couldn't be, I
thought I might as well work with what I had. Sometimes that meant acting a little braver than the situation required. Other times it meant fainting a little
more dramatically. At this time, I felt like I was
under a microscope. I wanted a little sympathy from
my mother and I wasn't getting it. And I resented
the hell out of it. I withdrew."

The sunshine ladies correctly interpreted her
withdrawal as a rejection of everything they sat for.
Her mother got caught in between. Unable to re-

strain herself, she began to criticize every move, slow or fast, that Angela made. For the first time in four years, Angela fought back, lashed back, while inside she crumbled.

Trying to explain herself once more, screaming for reason, she screamed in pain and doubled over. While her mother screamed into the telephone receiver for help—for Dowling—and shrieked "I wasn't responsible" into the air; while Angela waited, she told herself, "You don't look well."

She is used to it by now. Whenever she is having tests taken, in particular a lung scan, there are always more young men present than needed to do the job. But she notices one wearing dungarees, a dark polo, and old sneakers. Reading upside down over his clipboard as he signs his name, she can just make out T ... Tr. ... To his "What are you in here for," she replies, "I'm doing one to five years for pulmonary embolism." Tr ... Tred? ... —Fred!

In for another stretch. Dowling was her "accomplice"; their "target," the admissions office. It wasn't pulmonary embolism; it wasn't even the threat of a blood clot. The doctor had recognized the immediate necessity of getting her away from home, and had claimed an emergency that admissions would accept without challenge. It was a hiatus hernia, a stabbing, burning protrusion of a portion of the stomach through the diaphragm, that he had to explain to her.

She ran to see Eric, but someone else was sleeping in his bed. When did he get well, she wanted to know—"denial" on automatic pilot. Eric was dead—a brain tumor. " ... it's always something else." Where did that leave her?

Dowling couldn't talk about it. It had been several weeks and he couldn't tell her. The corners of his eyes were still red. As she was leaving his office, they both looked across the room at a recent photograph, enlarged, propped against a wall from a journal-strewn table. Eric, smiling. "You know, you should get a frame for that." She didn't try to see his answer. "One of these days."

Through dinner, through disbelieving night, it almost sang—the Ballad of Her Young Men. Eric was dead. ... Alan was dead. ... Jeff was gone. ... Russell was ...

She had to have another lung scan. Not because she was doing badly, but because she was doing so well. A pretty picture for Dowling's family album.

Still wearing dungarees, a light polo this time, sneakers again, "Fred" is in charge. While Angela holds her breath, out of habit, he seems more intent on scanning Camille, sister superior. Angela sighs as the test continues. He is called away for a moment, and before Angela can speak, Camille tells her she thinks he is playing up to her to get to Angela, and bets two tickets to any Broadway show on whether or not Angela can get him to ask her out. They both take a deep breath.

Dinner and a show. Only tonight it's a hospital dinner and a movie made for TV and she's alone, her stomach filling with caterpillars as she senses how young she is. Has she ever been out on a real date? The only door she can picture being held open for her is a door to the operating room; no one has ever kissed her good night. There are men, older men, that she's proud of—it's a strange world, where only the older men last—but they all belong to someone else. Unsweetened sixteen. Seventeen, eighteen, nineteen. Opened and closed and opened and opened wider and never really been kissed. Her young men ... never. Forever. Eric was dead. . . . Alan was dead. . . . Jeff gone and Russell . . . The dirge became doggerel. Eric was dead, Alan was dead. One down and two down, but then there was Fred. He looked "normal." She had a date to keep—no, to make! A bet to win.

She chooses the tightest sweater in her suitcase and lays it out, arms open, on the bed. It is her last chance. Camille had set a limit of a week to her wager, and it is the seventh day. It has taken time: first her stomach, then her make-up. Finally getting the right false eyelashes from "outside." Black opaque panty hose to cover her beige Jobst stockings. Camille winces as Angela screws herself into a tasteless pair of lavender hot pants. Never mind, she'll be waiting at the finish line. A deft tease of the hair and the contestant is ready.

She hasn't done all this for one man. To prove it, she gets permission to visit the blood lab; there she gets the full-dress "field-trip" treatment. Then, the X-ray lab, where she gets the "open-house" format.

No one is treating her like a patient. More visits, more confidence. Until she realizes she is running out of time and asks for Fred. A receptionist tells her there is no Fred in nuclear medicine. "Wait. You must mean Ted." Too far along to turn back, she takes what they offer. "Yeah, that's it, Ted."

She didn't expect a room full of men. And, damn her vanity, she wasn't wearing—never wore—her glasses. Well, she couldn't stand there in the doorway and call, "Fred, uh"—shaking her head—"Ted." So she took a stab, sensed he was *there*, or believed she did anyway.

The "Hi"s, "How are you"s, and "What's doin' "s consumed, he got her out of there, casually quickly, straight to the final lab of her journey, to nuclear "scanning."

"What are you all dressed up for?"

She told him all the places she had been that day.

"And you left me for last! Thanks a lot!"

"Saved you for last. You're ... " Welcome. Adorable. Ask me out.

"Want me to show you anything?"

"Sure ... do you have any daylight down here?"

"Not in these machines. Is it getting to you?"

"What?"

"You getting stir-crazy?"

Prison talk again. "Mm-hm. Doc says the warden would give me a pass, though. Lunch pass."

"That's terrific. You must be getting better."

"I can't eat the food here anymore."

"I know what you mean."

"Mm-hm." I'm not getting anywhere. Maybe I should offer him Camille.

"Well, you probably won't have to eat it much longer."

"Want to come and say hello to my sister?"

Camille isn't letting go of her place in the magazine story; she can't wait to get rid of him so she can coach her sister on what not to do with the next man. He has a lot to say: reading and holiday traffic and too much sun. Angela, a background voice on a local commercial, chants on about food. GOOD food, BAD food, TASTY food, yum. To please—no way of telling which—one of them, he asks, "Why don't you let me take you to lunch?" and doesn't laugh as Camille wants to jump up and down and howl at Angela's "I'm free tomorrow."

She's up at 6 a.m. Hair, nails, decisions. Ted is at twelve noon. On the way out of the hospital, she slips the hospital's identification band off of her wrist and puts it in her pocketbook. This is a date; she wants to feel normal. Besides, she lied about the pass.

It is a perfect day. Ted enters a sandwich shop while she waits outside, her face to the sun. They choose the right park bench, but why did he set the brown-paper bag between them? Tomorrow night are the fireworks . . . wouldn't it be nice? Inspired, he asks her what she thinks she is, a cherry bomb or a Roman candle. She replies, "I'm a sparkler"; he's convinced. He takes a sandwich from the bag and starts eating. That bag has come between them— there's only one sandwich! And he's not offering a bite! There goes her romantic afternoon. She's starving, but she won't say anything; she doesn't know how, and what the hell, she's "out," isn't she? But she's angry, and hurt. He doesn't want to get any germs; she's not normal. She can't hear what he's saying anymore. To get even, she tells him: she sneaked out.

Of course Camille was waiting. With her mouth full of fruit, candy, anything else she could find in the room, Angela despaired, pausing between "courses" only to add that in every other respect she had a good time. Camille's advice was to go out with the cheap bastard again. "What makes you so sure he'll ask me?" "You."

He asked her out for lunch again. She didn't start getting ready till eight, and she ate in her room. They went for a walk.

After several more no-lunch lunches, he asks if he can buy her a soda. The soda makes her heady; she asks if lunch ever includes food. While she pinches her straw, and he flattens his, they sort it out: "I thought you were only allowed to eat hospital food!"

They meet every day. Lunch, the lab, the lounge. Angela begins to fill the hours in between by doing volunteer secretarial work for one of the doctors in "the house." Her motive is selfish: she is removing herself one step farther from reality; the more she plays "doctor," which is what she is doing, the less of a patient she becomes.

She handles case histories, sometimes those of patients she knows, and discovers that a lot of them are sicker than they think they are. She never handles her own.

Dowling hasn't sent for her to congratulate her for the good work she's doing. Or to tell her that her stomach has healed.

"You're never in your room!"

"I've been doing more important things."

"I'm getting complaints."

"From whom?"

"From everybody. They can't get a test on you. They can't find you. You're never there."

"I'll rot if I stay there. Or go crazy!"

"I know how difficult it is for you. That's why I've let it go this far. But ... "

Time to find out.

"What do you mean?"

"I know you've been sneaking out. And I know why. I was trying to overlook it. But the staff is really upset, and I can't have that. Nor can I allow you to masquerade as an employee of the hospital. And wear someone else's badge when you come and go from here. If you get caught, I'm really going to hear it."

"Can't you take it?"

"Not for one patient, I won't. Even if it's you." Softening. "Angela, I need a little more time to take care of your stomach. To find the full extent of it. Don't make any waves."

"I can't stay in my room all day. Please!"

"You're going to have to. I'm sorry, but that's the way it is. And you're to stay inside the hospital."

"What if I won't?"

"We'll have to take all your clothes away from you."

"You'd do that to me!" He would. Put up a fight. "Fine. You do that to the little girl. Go ahead. Go ahead, you take all the little girl's clothes away and you do whatever you want to the little girl and you watch how fast she goes."

He gets nervous. "Goes? Goes where?"

"Goes. Just goes." Pleading. "I'm not doing this to cause trouble. I'm doing it to save myself. Can't you see that!"

"All right. All right. Keep your clothes. Tell your mother to bring you more if you want. But take it easy, will you?"

"If I give up my job . . . " The job is beginning to get to her anyway.

"That's a good start. You understand."

"Thank you." A look at the clock. "I have to go now. Will you excuse me?"

"Not yet. Stay put."

Another look at the clock. "Please."

"Lunch?"

"Mm-hm."

Wearily. "Go ahead. In the future, try and re-member that you're a patient."

Two inches above her height. "I'm not a patient!"

"Yes, you are. You're my patient."

Don't say it to him. "You're jealous." She said it.

*I*t had all the makings of a soap opera. Angela and Ted began to tell it that way to each other playfully.

Young hospital technician meets lovely young sickling in laboratory. He is charming, attentive, tells her he hopes to see her again but doesn't want to see her "down here." What he really wants to see, anywhere, is her healthy older sister. Who is married, happily, and doesn't want any part of him—for herself; she wants him for her sickly, younger sister. Technician and sickling sibling are thrown together. Exit older sister.

Enter the older man. The eminent doctor. She has always been infatuated with him. He has never declared himself. Now he has a rival. He sinks to the occasion. He tries to put an end to the budding relationship. He tries to part them and keep them apart. Will he succeed? Or will youth triumph? Tune in again . . .

Ted took her to a concert on the grounds of Central Park. This was their first evening date. Perhaps at night he would kiss her. He hadn't yet—because she was sick, she assumed—and she began to have her doubts about a future with any man. During the concert, he put his arm around her. He was beginning to relax from the uneasiness he felt being with a patient who, for the first time, was out illegally at night.

For the longest while, she doesn't move. She hates to break the mood by saying anything, but has to tell him she's due—a little overdue—for her medicine. No, she doesn't want something to wash it down with; she has to give herself an injection, and someone has to steady her heparin lock while she injects the syringe. It's as if she has just jabbed the needle into the bottom of his foot. His composure races his color to oblivion. It's at the height of the hard-drug craze, and even knitting needles are suspect. He commands her to let the song finish and then exit unceremoniously with him. Damn it. She doesn't want to leave and she shouldn't delay the shot. "But you don't understand...." And he claps his hand over her mouth. And again. As they weave their way between the huddled bodies on the ground, the next selection, "I've Got You Under My Skin," begins ... and repeats and repeats in his pounding ear.

On the edge of the Park, they share a nervous shot, a nervous laugh, a nervous kiss. For Angela, the ride back is a bumpy one. "I hope he doesn't hurt me.... If he walks out on me, it won't be the end of the world. I won't die.... I'll kill him!"

Next installment. She re-examines the doctor. After all, he is the man who saved her life. More than once. How can she not love him for that? For his part, he has never been more endearing. And his secretary has said things about his feelings that convince Angela that he loves her. Nevertheless, he has terrible things to say about the young man.

The young man has terrible things to say about the doctor. But he's such a handsome young man....

At the end of their second evening together, Angela is about to receive her second kiss from Ted. This one is really important to her, because somewhere in that kiss she hopes to find, by hearing or feeling or something, if it's love. Or isn't. The kiss ended, she has solved nothing; has been distracted, decoyed—is this normal?—by a hand on her backside.

Back in her room, she decides: I'm gonna get this guy to marry me. I may not love him now, but I just know I will. Through the night her heart selects the little boy in the man, and expands upon recognizing that the little boy is unhappy. Two little children in grownups' clothes are complaining to each other that they never had a normal childhood: she's never been given any responsibility, and he's had too much thrust upon him. Neither one free. She begins thinking: Maybe I can make one person happy. By morning she is loving him.

We continue.... The young girl's upbringing has instilled in her two inflexible principles: first, no sex before marriage (she's had almost too much cooperation in upholding this one!); and, second, you love one man. She is in danger of eternal damnation. She loves one too many....

And disagrees with both, increasingly. Dowling blames Ted for every minor setback on her chart. Complains that he isn't good for her, doesn't take proper care of her. She begins to receive his daily litany in icy silence. Ted tells her that Dowling is a terrible doctor, is making terrible decisions in her case. She shouts back in defense of Dowling. Her mother, on the telephone, adds her voice to the dissonance: she doesn't like him; true, she's never met him, but that won't make any difference.... Camille says he has a mustache.

Enter a new character, the young doctor. Young

Dr. Rogers. Very handsome. In flagrant pursuit. But the girl's pulse doesn't quicken for him. She's got both hands full as it is. The young doctor finds himself irresistible, isn't accustomed to being rebuffed. . . .

Ted and Angela were on the town—their second or third disco that night. He ordered another soda for her and another glass of Chablis for himself. She was amused by the white wine—her family drank red—and asked, once more, for a taste. Neither of them knew if it was a good idea, but he gave in and gave her one. When he excused himself and left the table for a few minutes, she took a larger sip; and when he returned, while his head was turned away watching the dancers, she took a few more. His drink went so fast he ordered another. They both left unsteadily. They were singing, trying to harmonize, when they ran into young Dr. Rogers on Madison Avenue. Alone. Staggered right into him.

The following morning, first order, Rogers stormed Dr. Dowling's office to lodge his complaint, unaware how deep-seated and unresolvable were Dowling's problems with her. Failing to get the reaction or action he expected, Rogers broke for Angela's room, where she was entertaining an early visitor—Ted. Rogers ordered Ted out of the room, drew the curtain around her bed, and jumped into it and on top of her. The wrestling must have jarred him to his senses; within minutes he concluded with a stream of obscenities and removed himself, from bed, from room, from her bedside forever.

Ted was wild. He wanted to go after him, doctor or

no, job be damned. For days, he boiled about it, while she blew on it and tried to get him to forget it. She didn't want anyone fighting over her, although it sure felt good to have someone who wanted to. He was jealous—no, possessive. No man had ever been that about her before! On and on he ranted—mine . . . my girl . . . us.

But he hadn't mentioned love. And it was unlikely that he would propose before the mention of it. Angela wondered if she might . . . but no. She did the next best thing. She got well enough to leave the hospital. Dowling dismissed her with a warning: This man will never accept the responsibility of taking care of you.

Ted was waiting. Though their families were miles apart, their houses were close to each other—practically the same neighborhood. His, Brighton Beach, bordered hers, Gravesend. "Brighton and Gravesend—what a combination! First stop, Gravesend!" He drove up to the house slowly, parked carefully. He went inside with her and, with a little charm and his endearingly scrawny mustache, removed any objection Mrs. Ambrosia had to him. All her father would say was "Be home early!"— followed by precisely *how* early.

Meeting his parents was more difficult for both of them. He had never brought a girl home before. Ambrosia! Ted's mother hadn't survived a concentration camp to hand her son over to a Gentile. Ted's father, self-made man and self-styled heavy, envisioned a bright future for his son that didn't leave any room for catering to a sick girl.

And where would the money come from? She thought of that before anyone else had brought it up; but they were sure to. Dowling saw to it that the initial grant continued to cover her major medical expenses, but she was still expensive, she knew that; she had seen the strain on her father. Nevertheless, Ted had a salary . . . and a career.

With Dowling, Jehovah and Christ, and the bill collector declaring eminent domain on the oxygen surrounding her, she decided to coax matters along. She and Ted were going swimming. Under her clothes she wore a skimpy two-piece bathing suit, which she had purposely chosen so that he would see her scars. It was a big thing to her. On the way to the beach, he mumbled something, she said what, he said nothing, and she wondered if she had heard right—I love you. As they bobbed up and down in the water, as they called to each other and laughed, the words, like a fish in the mouth of a seal, started to slip away from her. He said what, but she retrieved them just in time and answered nothing and pulled the next wave over herself. Out of their wet things and walking away from the beach, she asked what he thought of the scars and he said what scars. On the way home he said it and she said it—I love you—and they decided aloud to get married. They hugged and kissed and splashed a few tears on each other. The next thing she said was "If we're really going to get married, tomorrow we get the ring, the hall, and the furniture." They shook on it.

. . . The young girl's mother had wanted her to marry a doctor. Not for the usual reasons, but because he would already know everything about her and how to take care of her. The young man's father had wanted his son to be a doctor. But not to take care of one sick girl. The girl's own doctor was only intent on taking care of the life he had saved, and gravely in doubt about the other man's ability to do so. Boy meets girl, boy almost loses girl, boy gets girl. Once they had won, had made the commitment, they secretly wondered whether they could make it or not. . . .

Mrs. Ambrosia's reaction to the blurted news of marriage was "If you're really getting married, tomorrow you get the ring, the hall, and the furniture."

She was engaged to be; among the living.

She was going to be somebody new. Somebody she knew she would like better than the someone she had been. Someone everybody would like better. She had prayed and she had dreamed, she had sweated between overstarched sheets; and now she had it—the chance to start all over again.

A new name. She tried it on for hours at a time. Mrs. Ted Rubel. Mrs. Theodore Rubel. Mrs. T. A. Rubel. Angela Ambrosia Rubel. Angela Rubel. She couldn't decide; she liked them all. She would use one for her stationery and another for her hospital records and another for her checks. Her checks! She had never written one and didn't know how, but she had seen Camille's name with Tony's on their checks, and she thought it was the "niftiest thing" to have one's name on one's checks in case people couldn't read the signature.

She left a note for her mother and signed it "Mrs. Ted Rubel." Her mother left one in return: "Will Mrs. Rubel tell Mrs. Ambrosia's daughter Angela to clean her room when she gets home?" When Angela left a message for Ted at the hospital she would say it was his fiancée calling. She almost embedded two fingernails in the receiver when a receptionist asked, "Would you like to leave a name?"

She could see the humor in most situations, but her in-laws-to-be left little room for laughter. She was somebody new, all right, so new that they refused to acknowledge her existence. It was bad enough that no one ever recognized her voice on the phone, but a lot worse when to their query "Who's calling?" she would reply, as warmly as she could, "Hi! It's Angela," and mother, father, or kid sister would respond with "Who?"

All right, so everyone didn't love her. She felt so new that she never doubted that she would win their love in time. You can't dislike a newborn, even when she cries, and Angela wasn't crying. Not for a minute. Angela Ambrosia-soon-to-be-Rubel was dauntless. She was going to be married. Twice! First, the way Camille was married. In the same church. In the same gown. In the same reception hall. Then the way Mr. and Mrs. Rubel were married, the way their ancestors were married, whatever way that was, it didn't matter. Not to the future Mrs. Angela Ambrosia Rubel.

It mattered to the Rubels. They took no interest

in the ring, the hall, or the furniture. They wanted no wedding, no ceremony, but if they had to have one, they wanted only one ceremony, and that would take place under the *chuppah*, the traditional canopy of a Jewish wedding.

Angela was unaware of the reasons for their resistance—and was to remain unaware of the reasons for the reasons for a long time to come—when she went on a fence-mending expedition to the Rubels. What she was aware of was the increasing pressure on Ted. Little by little, the Rubels were succeeding where all else had failed—if not depriving her of life itself, as her illness had so often threatened to do, then threatening to deprive her of Ted. It was just what the man who had repeatedly saved her life, Dowling, had also attempted. And exactly as Angela had taken her fury with Dowling out on Ted, now he was letting his shame and frustration with his parents spill over into their relationship. It was a relationship she meant to protect at all costs. Pride, to her, was something you displayed in the operating room. This was preservation.

Angela and Mr. Rubel walked around the yard together. She asked for his objections, and he gave several, but she had trouble believing any of them. "He's too young." "He's going to be a doctor." " . . . doesn't know what he wants." She tried to answer them, calmly, but of course there were no answers, and even as she talked, she started to think and couldn't restrain herself from thinking: I've never known or heard of a Jewish girl named Angela. He continued. "You're very young." " . . . haven't known each other long enough." "No money." She asked herself: Is it that basic? And aloud she asked, "Is it because I'm not Jewish?" And he said, "You don't know what we've been through!" And she said, "You don't know what I've been through!" She said the wrong thing. Before she could resolve the one issue, he was on to another.

"You are a sick girl."

"But I'm better now!"

He shook it off, right and left, with a head that suddenly looked grayer and wiser than it had looked just a few moments before. And sadder. She respected that. Unaccountably, she shivered. It silenced her.

Amid the confusion in her mind, a distant siren went off again, and she wondered if he—like everyone else, it sometimes seemed—knew something she didn't know.

*D*owling had promised that when she turned twenty-one, or if she was getting married before she turned twenty-one, he would explain to her what it was she had. She was only nineteen and she didn't intend to wait two years to get married. Now, with all this new uncertainty in her life, she had to know—to pin down—something.

"I walked into his office like Mary Tyler Moore—you know, Mary Tyler Moore doesn't sweat; neither does Angela Ambrosia." She was going to ask him what she had and he was going to tell her, and if she asked him if it was anything like leukemia, he was going to give her an emphatic no. But while she was asking, she would ask anyway, because "there was Ted now . . . another whole person involved here . . . and he had to know what the full story was with me. And the next step in my growing up was to tell him."

She walked into Dowling's office and asked what she had, and he answered but didn't tell her. So she asked if she had leukemia. There it was. And he answered, "Yes, Angela, you do."

She felt as if her insides were anesthetized. She held everything in. She heard him saying, "Do you really think this guy wants to marry you?" And thought: God, how could he ask me this question now? But she answered, "Yes, of course he wants to marry me." But, of course, she didn't know. Once again, she felt she didn't know anything.

Dowling, who knew everything—except what kind of man Ted was—said, "For your sake, I hope so. But be prepared." For her sake. Then she asked him about having children—really a harder question for her—and he said he doubted very much whether she would ever be able to have a child. That devastated her. That threatened her life more than the leukemia! He explained that the drugs she had been on were gene-altering and the only thing she might be capable of conceiving would be a monster.

Now she didn't know what to feel or how to feel. She just knew that she had to go downstairs and tell the man she loved that she wasn't going to marry him. And she wanted to spare this other man she loved, Dowling, because she knew how much having to tell her must have hurt him. So she didn't have any reaction. Just a little laugh and a giggle and a "See you next week" as if it were just another weekly visit. But all the while she kept running it through her brain that she was going downstairs to tell Ted that she wasn't going to marry him.

There were twice as many steps on the stairs as there had been before. But she was careful. There was no sound. And the walls kept getting darker and colder.

Ted's office was the last door on the left. He was the only one there. "I didn't pass a living soul. I would have noticed the living." He asked, as he always asked at such times, what Dowling had to say. She answered with what was filling her mind: she thought they should call off the wedding. Ted jumped up and she knew she couldn't run away from it— maybe him, but not the words. "He said I have leukemia." "Don't talk, don't say anything," and he moved to hold her, and for the first time since she had become ill, she moved away. As if she might catch something. He reached out with words, his, brushing aside hers and Dowling's. "We love each other. Why shouldn't we get married?" She told him about the impossibility of having children. He tried to talk and she wouldn't let him. He tried to keep her from leaving, but she prevailed. "I'm walking out that door. Don't call me back ... because if you call me back, I don't know if I can keep on walking. For your sake ... " She trailed off. And she left.

"I remember the hallway closing in on me. And choking me. And I remember—I can still remember distinctly—the feeling of death. Behind me Ted's voice asking, and then, as my steps got faster and faster, pleading with me not to go. I remember the sound of each foot on the floor and his voice and the echo of his voice. 'I was never happy before you!' And I looked behind me and he was crying. 'Please.' And I hesitated. 'Angela?' And I asked myself how I could make someone I loved so much so unhappy. And he cried out, 'I knew! I knew you had leukemia!' And breaking down, 'But I couldn't tell you!' ''

And she started running toward him and she saw herself in his arms and she was safe. If she could just get into his arms! And she got there. He held her head to his chest and patted it and said, "If you give me a month, even a day, you'll be giving me a lifetime of happiness."

*G*ott *in Himmel*—an invalid! Terminal! No children—no son to extend the Rubel line, not even a half-Jewish one ... after all they'd been through ... God forbid! The pressure at home on Ted was unbearable, so much so that when it built up beyond endurance, when he cursed his father with language that shocked him even as it came out of his mouth, he wasn't sure if he was forced out of his house, or thrown out.

Ted appeared at the Ambrosias' back door in tears. Because it was nighttime and because even if it had been the beginning instead of the end of the usual long, hard day, Mr. Ambrosia could never have found the right words, he quietly withdrew to the basement, from which he soon emerged with a pair of his own freshly laundered pajamas, which he had ironed so that they would be warm and comforting to the boy. The next day, Ted moved in with a cousin, but his heart never left that house.

If Angela had been sleepwalking up to this point, she was awake now and, with eyes wide open, was looking over her shoulder. The reality that Ted had never outrun—had, to his credit, never tried to outrun—was closing in on her. Loving her family as much as she did, she saw how great was Ted's sacrifice, how potentially destructive was each obstacle, how long the odds. They both saw that you can't fight people the way you fight germs—you can't radiate prejudice or anesthetize ignorance. Had their courage been an illusion? From the moment they had made their commitment to each other, events had propelled them forward at such a dizzying speed that what lay ahead for them—whether they could make it or not—frightened them into action.

Ted made an appointment to see Dowling, and was kept waiting for an hour. Although their meeting did nothing to enlighten Ted beyond what he already knew, and helped not at all to clear the air, Dowling saw him to the door, apologized for keeping him waiting, and recommended they meet again. Ted thanked him for his apology and made another appointment, for which he didn't show up. He called to apologize, explaining that pressing hospital business had interfered, and made another appointment. For which he showed up, on time, and was once again kept waiting. It became a pattern: Dowling keeping Ted waiting, Ted not showing up—two grown professional men acting like children.

Round 2: Dowling made a great display of locking up his files because Ted was an "employee" of the hospital. When he found out, Ted contended that Dowling was afraid that someone who knew something about medicine might discover how ineptly he had handled Angela's case. Unable and unwilling to believe any such accusation but appalled by Dowling's irascibility, Angela gestured wildly at the filing cabinet while informing Dowling that it was obvious that it was she whom he wanted to keep under lock and key.

And so it continued, Dowling and Ted striking out at each other, Dowling and Angela striking back at each other, until Christmas, 1971, interceded and mellowed all three contenders. When Dowling ran into Angela on an unscheduled visit to the hospital and she told him she was meeting Ted to go Christmas shopping, he responded with "Don't waste your time with him. Come with me. You'll have more fun." Angela knew better; nothing the doctor could do could match the Christmas Ted was about to give her.

They had already chosen her engagement ring, but she didn't know when she was going to receive it. The jeweler they found—unexpectedly, in a tiny storefront in a Sheepshead Bay shopping center— had been evasive about everything: the cost of the diamond, baguettes, setting; the size of the deposit;

when he could have it ready for them. But over the course of their visits, he had become so friendly, so interested in them, that they discontinued their comparison shopping and returned continually to him. He would serve them coffee or tea and listen with great concern while they told him about their hopes for the future, about Angela's health, about their problems.

When they finally pinned him down to a price on the diamond they had chosen, it was half what they expected it to be. Still he wouldn't take their money—not until they took the stone, please!, and had it appraised by three or four of the jewelers they had previously seen. Each of the other jewelers told the couple that the stone was worth twice as much as he was asking. When they returned to their Santa, saying very little lest they say the wrong thing, he filled the silent void by nodding his head from side to side, declaring "You drive a hard bargain," and threw in the baguettes and setting for nothing.

Angela knew Mrs. Rubel had some small stones from an old brooch that she wanted reset for her two daughters. Angela saw it as a way of bringing Ted and his parents together again. She didn't want to be the wedge driven between them and she wasn't convinced by his seeming indifference to them—you don't just walk away from family! She called—the hell with the "Who?" at the other end—and, after a few awkward opening cordialities, told Mrs. Rubel enthusiastically about their "find." In all likelihood, Mrs. Rubel saw it "as a way," too. She reacted with

101

equal enthusiasm and a date was made. That evening Angela told Ted, as quickly as she could, that his mother was coming with them that Saturday.

In the car, they spoke about jewelry and the weather. Angela had only to look at them, not listen, to know she had done the right thing. They were mother and son.

Ted's mother knew exactly what she wanted and she told the jeweler so. She was restrained but pleasant, never overbearing. The jeweler was restrained as well, but extraordinarily attentive to Mrs. Rubel's order. The man seemed uneasy in her presence. After they left the shop, she didn't speak bargains or settings. Her only comment was "Those aren't the hands of a jeweler." Angela kicked herself with her high-mindedness and thought: What a tough cookie!

*C*hristmas Eve at the Ambrosias' was an elegant affair this year. The whole family was together and they had dressed handsomely and gift-wrapped lavishly for the occasion. The warm light from the fireplace lapped up and down and around their legs like so many nuzzling puppies. Home for the holidays!—Angela looked upon the scene with great satisfaction. The stately manicured evergreen was spangled with satin balls suspended from velvet ribbons and gleaming with tinsel. Too much tinsel, Angela thought, that was Ted's doing; he was so nervous, poor dear, it wasn't even his holiday and it seemed to mean so much to him!

Then he dropped the hint. All that glitters is not gold, but one thing that glitters in that tree is eighteen precious carats. Angela combed the tree with the careful fervor of an archaeologist. She wanted that ring. Her fingers separated the branches, sifted through the rows of pine needles as her eyes darted and her heart pounded until ... she touched it, she saw it, she had it. Slipping it off the little branch about a foot above her, she held it between the cupped fingers of both hands and stared, and wept, and laughed. As Ted and the others stared and wept and laughed with her, without moving. Then she put it on, and kissed it and the knuckle above it, and then threw her arms around Ted and kissed him —hard. And it ran through her mind that she had never kissed a man on the mouth in front of her father before.

She held her left hand under the light and they drank champagne. She held it by the firelight and she and Ted drank a quiet toast to each other. All through midnight Mass she rubbed it, breathed on it, and rubbed it again, held it a thousand different distances from her nose and inspected it. By the time she went to bed, she had put the ring under every light, fluorescent or otherwise, in the house.

As soon as the holidays were over, they returned to the jewelry store to pick up Mrs. Rubel's belongings and to inquire about a wedding band, but the jeweler had apparently had a good holiday, too, because he wasn't open for business that day. Nor the next. Nor did he open at any time the following week—or, in fact, ever again. It seemed that he had very dubious credentials and very questionable associates and had absconded with a fortune in deposits and other people's jewelry, including Mrs. Rubel's, leaving behind no remnant of the enterprise that had been in existence, no trace of himself, and only one ring—which, out of some not quite dried-up wellspring of humanity, he had sold at half its market value.

"*L*ife was unreal. And confusing. My religion and my disease combined to make death all too real to me. But parents who didn't behave like parents, who disowned children who'd never had a childhood and weren't children anymore . . . Jewelers who weren't jewelers, who gave away jewelry . . . Unreal!"

She was finally going to see what a Jewish wedding looked like. An ex-girlfriend of Ted's was getting married and Angela and Ted were invited to the wedding. He insisted Angela wear white. "I told him only the bride wears white, but he said that wasn't true at a Jewish wedding and he wanted me to wear white."

She couldn't wait to get there. She was going to imagine herself as the bride. "The only thing I knew about Jewish ceremonies was circumcision, and I knew they couldn't circumcise the bride." Ted kept taking his time.

"When we finally arrived at the wedding hall, I didn't see another soul. Ted opened the door and it was pitch dark and I said, 'We can't go in now, we're too late.' I was so nervous about doing the wrong thing in front of the Jewish community—I was sure that they all knew each other and that my future in-laws would hear about it from every single one of them. But Ted said, 'Shut up! This is what a Jewish ceremony is like. It always starts out in the dark.'" In the dark, he couldn't see the disappointment, the despair on her face, but she was miserable. She thought they would have to get married in the dark. In all her fantasies of her wedding day she had never imagined herself being married in the dark! Standing there, unable to see her trembling hand before her, she still couldn't imagine it.

Then the lights went on and she couldn't see, but she heard all these voices chanting a Jewish word that almost sounded English and it seemed as if it were coming in her direction, and she thought: That's it, now I've done it—late or white ... I'm sorry, I'm really sorry ... please don't tell my in-laws. Louder and closer, and it sounded like "surprise" and she thought she was imagining familiar faces, and she thought she saw ... "Then I saw my mother coming toward me, and my sister, and lots of people who wouldn't tell on me. And it hit me—this is a shower, my shower!"

Weddings that weren't weddings. As if the prospect of two weddings—one familiar and one "still in the dark"—wasn't unreal enough to a girl who considered herself lucky to be getting married once, "Imagine the preposterousness of losing my virginity twice—once for my husband's friends and

105

once for my family. I'd better explain. Ted and I weren't sleeping together. I had a lot of hang-ups about sex and he was very patient with me. But he was concerned that his friends, who became my friends, wouldn't understand. Which I didn't quite understand, but tried. I had been brought up to believe that premarital sex was a sin. My father, I knew without having to ask him, still believed it. So did the fathers of the other girls, I was willing to bet. But now it seemed that no premarital sex, although not condemned by my church or theirs, was worse. Still, I couldn't . . . so we lied.

"To our friends we 'were,' which was very good for me because it actually made me feel a little more worldly and a little less frightened. And while I knew that I 'wasn't,' thanks to my reliable imagination I was able to believe that Ted—at the same time!—'was.' I was glad I was going to have a husband who was only a little older and only a little more experienced than I was. I thought it would be nice if we kind of grew together, and would have been afraid of anyone I considered 'too experienced'—Dowling, whom I had wanted for so long, for instance. Somehow, I associated 'very experienced' with pain. But I did want my husband to know something, so that we wouldn't stand there like idiots or get hurt trying."

Her engagement extended twelve months, over a period when the world expects young girls to pass smoothly into young women. She had hurled herself onto the conveyor belt very near the end of the line, and while she held her head up proudly to accept the finishing touches, she was at the same time frantically trying to assemble the rest of the woman—herself—beneath.

"I spent most of the year trying to be someone else instead of finding 'me.' " She was Natalie Wood in everything—*Splendor in the Grass, Marjorie Morningstar, Love with the Proper Stranger*—as she imagined her in movies she hadn't even seen. When she was alone and trying to sort things out, she felt like Alice in Wonderland; when caught between her father and Ted, she was Cinderella, dressed for the ball but obliged to be home by midnight. Only, like Natalie Wood, she couldn't lose the glass slipper. "Not without a great deal of anguish. Not even to Ted, my prince, my fiancé."

With less than a month to go before their wedding, they began to fix up the apartment that would be theirs but that they were not allowed to be alone in after dark, father's orders. A few days before the wedding, on their way back to her house after an afternoon of cleaning, they stopped at a neighborhood fair, and while they threw an extra ball or two at some milk bottles, it grew dark—barely. Papa, in a state of apoplexy, shot out of the house and over to the apartment, which was only six minutes away. Fortunately, by the time he returned home, Angela and Ted were sitting there on the couch in the living room ... with a full arm's distance between them.

She was beginning to count the days and nights and hours till "blast-off." She knew she was going to make it—there wasn't a weapon or disease on earth

107

that could keep her from that altar. But a new fear was creeping in on her: something might happen to Ted. She began to "preserve" him. She prayed for him and she made sure he got enough rest; she called to make sure he ate lunch and she called his apartment to wake him every morning. With little more than two days and two nights, fifty-four hours, to go, he wasn't answering his phone. She knew he was a sound sleeper, but nobody could sleep through two hours of constant ringing, and she just knew he was ill, or something worse. Her father had already left for work, so she called Ted's father and told him how frightened she was, and he picked her up right away.

They rang Ted's doorbell and they banged on his front door. They woke everyone in bed on the floor. Everyone but Ted. The superintendent let them in, and there was Ted, cuddled up, grinning, sound asleep. Still unconvinced, she put her hand gently on his cheek and just like that! he opened his eyes and said, "Oh, hi!" She was so angry that she picked up a slipper, and before he knew what had hit him—on the backside—she was out of that apartment and on her way home.

"Nevertheless, I got it from my father! 'You went to a man's apartment!' " Being that she was going to marry the man in . . . it was now forty-five hours . . . and that she was with the man's father didn't make any difference. "Unreal."

*I*t was a beautiful day that would turn nasty—the day before their wedding. Their weddings. Two sets of invitations had been printed and sent out, one announcing both weddings and one—necessitated by Ted's father—announcing only the second, the Jewish ceremony. He wasn't to know that there would be any other.

Angela and Ted were all dressed up, on their way to a cocktail party not, to their nervous relief, in their honor. Among tomorrow's uncertainties was Mr. Rubel's attendance. At the second wedding, the one they had so carefully arranged to look like the only wedding to him! He had repeatedly threatened not to show up. For Ted's sake, for the sake of their life together, Angela had to have him there.

The idea came from both of them. Right now, while they looked so good, so innocent together, was a good time to visit his parents. An "insurance" visit. The conversation began with Mr. Rubel telling Angela how pretty she looked. Then, while Ted helped his mother with something in the kitchen, Angela and Mr. Rubel—ritually, it began to seem—went for another walk around the yard. It was their metaphor: pacing the perimeters as they sought to mend fences.

She asked if he was coming to the wedding. He was still struggling with the answer. "Why," she asked, "why do you want to hurt us so much?" And he was genuinely shocked. "I don't want to hurt anybody!" And then he told her. . . .

Both he and Lillian Rubel had been "buried" in the concentration camps, she for seven years. He couldn't talk about himself, so he talked about her. She had been a nurse; yes, he responded to Angela's surprise, a nurse . . . and, meaningfully, "she knows a great deal." She was very, very beautiful, he reminisced, and the combination of her brains and her beauty was her salvation. He spoke without emotion, and Angela understood: you don't show your emotions, it's too risky. She had learned the same thing, and she realized that what she had always felt from them, what had kept her coming back for more, was the undercurrent of emotion—of pain and fear and despair—that pulled her irresistibly along. And she could hide hers no longer—the tears trickled. This was not the Christians being thrown to the lions, this was now! She had been pulled through life by years of hands—black, yellow, red, and white; all religions and all nationalities—all had nursed her. But these people had suffered the unspeakable at the hands of neighbors-turned-foreigners. She wanted him there tomorrow for her sake and his. But she had to be firm. She told him; and she told him, "Your times of suffering are over. I may have to go through it for the rest of my life."

September 3, 1972.

Both sides of the street outside the Ambrosia house were filled with friends and neighbors waiting to see their "little angel" as a bride. She emerged, autumn flowing from the horn of summer, her skin a golden harvest tone against her white lace gown and her burnished auburn hair. She knew she was beautiful that day: everything she felt inside was right there on her face. A few gasps of appreciation and they began to applaud, and then cheer, and then—although this was only the beginning of the day, they couldn't wait—to celebrate: to throw confetti and pass around cups of champagne.

She noted that it was hot, and thought about Ted sitting in their apartment, where the men were meeting, fully dressed in his tuxedo since noon, with his fingers clasped together on his lap like a model schoolboy in class, as Philip had found him and subsequently called, just as she was getting out of bed, to describe him. She remembered their first lunch date when she was up and ready at dawn, and laughed. Poor Ted was so nervous. She wasn't too sure of tonight, could never be too sure of the future, but right now she knew exactly what she was doing.

In the limousine, on the way to the church, she remembered the only other limo rides she'd ever taken, when the limo was a black ambulance taking her to the hospital. It almost started again, the litany: Eric was dead, and Alan was dead ... and Jeff? And Russell? No! ... She was getting married! Today she really was Cinderella and there was no midnight. She had felt like a princess when her bridal party had poured into her room and each girl had lent a hand to the finishing touches. Today she was getting married. Eric again. "I won't ever get married," she vowed, "unless you're at my wedding"; and he promised, "You got a deal." Oh, God! ... Well, at least one of us made it *this* far.

111

Her father had been irritable earlier today. Could she do anything wrong now? Could he forbid her to have her wedding night? They were at the church and there was Daddy, giving her his hand, that steadying hand, helping her out of the car. "I love you," they said to each other.

They entered, and there was the music she had waited for so long to hear played for her. Everybody was grinning, grinning. As she walked down the aisle, she could just make Ted out. He was grinning, too, but she knew he was tense. He had suffered a last-minute case of nerves last night, had sworn not to let anybody interfere with this day, would let his parents have it, or her parents. . . . He had acted like a spoiled child, and she could have killed him!

They stood in front of the altar together, listening to the priest. They would both be glad when it was over. When it came time for her father to give her to the groom, he was slow, so slow he drew laughter, to let go. The priest spoke to the congregation beyond them. There were only two people left and they looked at each other, and at the right moment they sprang open, and laughed, and kissed unselfconsciously.

She had finally lived out a fantasy. Something that happens to normal girls. She was married.

Wasn't she? She still had another wedding to go to. Up the aisle and into the car, waving and throwing kisses anywhere. "I am almost Mrs. T. H. Rubel."

A mile from the church, the limousine pulled over and Ted and the driver removed the "Just Married" signs and the confetti while she picked and shook and brushed the rice from her head without moving a single hair. Car and occupants immaculate, they proceeded, late, to the hall. Mrs. Rubel was waiting outside for them. Mr. Rubel was inside! Her welcoming words were "What did you come in the same car for? All the trouble we went to, and you messed it up!" Perhaps they had. Ted said, "Let me handle this" to the new Mrs. Rubel, and to the other, "Mother, shut up!" Angela made her way through the crowd mumbling and moaning about the stupid limousine driver who had picked them up together. It was all coming slowly down to earth.

It sank a little deeper before it came up again. In the rooms set aside for last-minute preparations, Ted, amid the confusion of a subterfuge that necessitated two of everything, remembered to return the ring to the best man so that it could be given again, remembered to receive the bride as if she were being given for the first time, remembered the second marriage license . . . which he had forgotten. For the next half-hour, while the Gentiles looked at the latest arrivals at the party, the Jews, on whom they were one up for the day on weddings, and the Jews looked anxiously at Mr. Rubel, the doubtful starter who they feared might not become a finisher, Angela paced, Ted perspired, and the license was retrieved.

The second wedding was a fairy tale for her. Inquisitive faces she'd never seen, Ted's relatives from all over the world, profiles she observed on shoulders and backs that made their heads seem larger and holier. Palms and ferns, palms along the footpath, and there at the end—resplendent royal purple, blue, red—the canopy, a castle in a Biblical kingdom for a little girl, the royal bride.

The rabbi, with the rich voice of a cantor, and a young soprano became a full choir as they received them with "Sunrise, Sunset"; and as they intoned, "Is this the little girl I carried . . . ?" all those who had carried her in their thoughts, and their hearts, and all those who would from this day on carry her with them through life—all those wept.

There is, in the Jewish wedding ceremony, that moment near the culmination when the groom steps on and breaks a wineglass wrapped in cloth to remind Jewish people everywhere that even on such a sweet occasion as a wedding they must not forget the bitter days of their history and the destruction of their temples; and on such a sweet occasion as a wedding, where the bitter mixes with the sweet, the wine is made all the sweeter in contrast to the bitter vessel that must, yet cannot, contain it. When the ceremony had carried everyone to this moment, Ted stomped on the parcel at his foot, Angela loudly proclaimed "Mazel tov," and, as the wave momentarily receded, bride and groom floated into each other's arms.

Her men got to her first: Daddy . . . Tony . . . Philip; her father-in-law, Dad, for now he was one of the men in her life—she knew how hard it had been for him, and she was grateful; Dowling, whom she was at peace with and whom she thanked without feeling the need to explain herself, and who, beaming, confided that he had already given himself a little pat on the back.

More men: her Uncle Tony, and her godfather, Paul. And her nephew—she turned and there was Ziggy, Ted's six-year-old brother, who had been one of the ushers, and she said, "Come here, Ziggy, let me give you a great big hug. . . . You were so wonderful, you didn't make one mistake, you were perfect!" and he stumbled and the Coke he was drinking ran up and then down the front of her gown. As the color drained from her face, so quickly that it looked as if the color itself was what was running down the front of her gown, she excused herself, adjourned with Ted to a private room, and screamed. And then they laughed and howled and shook their heads in disbelief. It had, after all, finally succumbed to the laws of nature and come down to earth.

If a Rubel had sunk them, a Rubel would save them. Ted's sister, Dinah, had once heard a story about a boy who discovered, several hours before the big dance at a campus weekend, that the rented tux he had brought with him had a fist-sized hole in one leg, and rather than disappoint or embarrass the girl he was there to escort, he painted his leg with black shoe polish. Dinah delicately experimented with her white eye make-up, applying a dab and rubbing it in a little, and applying another and not rubbing it in so much, and it seemed to be working. So she applied it all, went out and rounded up all the eye-white she could get her hands on, and painted and smeared and brushed until the stain was completely coated and Angela felt bride-white again.

It was only a matter of time, the amount of time Angela and Ted had been absent, for the solemnity to give way to hilarity. They thought for a moment that they had walked in on somebody else's reception—cheering, singing, screaming—but it was the Ambrosia-Rubel affair, all right, just your typical Italian-Jewish wedding, they agreed, and they fell right into step, each willing to bet that his or her side of the family was louder. They danced, he drank, they cut the cake. Angela insisted Ted taste it, at least the icing!, although he couldn't tolerate sweets. This was their wedding cake! Toast followed toast, and they waltzed and changed partners, and changed again, and again, and when the toasting got back to them, she couldn't find Ted. No one could find Ted, until someone reported him found—in the men's room, throwing up.

Oh, no, the cake! Their wedding cake! His family became concerned, excessively, she thought, and as she made her way out of the hall—again—she thought, somewhat remorsefully: He's supposed to be taking care of me!

Their wedding cake! On their wedding day! With their night still to come! She couldn't believe it. This was . . . well, damn . . . the icing on the cake was the icing on the cake!

The bellboy leered. Didn't he? She had been nervous, but the sight of the bed, strangely enough, relaxed her. While she made the room hers, Ted brushed his teeth for the sixth, and then, if she heard correctly,

116

the seventh time. While she got ready for bed, she called to him, six or seven times, "Don't fall asleep!" Her nightgown was made to order, what she had always pictured herself in, long white satin trimmed with white feathers, her wedding gift from Ted. She emerged somewhat stiffly, tried to relax underneath all that show, in front of him. He turned off the TV and appraised: "It's a damn shame." "What is—the gown? You don't like it?" "All that money I spent, and I'm going to rip it off you in two seconds!"

An hour and two seconds later, as she lay in his arms, she muttered, "Damn, Ted, if they'd given me you years ago, I'll betcha I never would've gotten sick at all."

She called home in the morning. She would be leaving them soon enough—tomorrow, perhaps, when she went on her honeymoon—but she hadn't left them yet. Her father couldn't deal with it so soon, not even on the phone, but her mother asked, "How was it?" It. "Mom, there are feathers all over the room!"

"*T*his was it! Me, Angela, the kid from Brooklyn, on a 747 on her way to Europe. I clung to Ted, dug my fingers into his arm, as the engines struggled to lift us off the ground. But once in the air, I was free, free! I had never been anywhere.... Now I was bound for everywhere. I walked up and down the aisle—aisles, two of them! I looked out of a dozen different windows. I spent five unnecessary minutes in the cutest little bathroom I'd ever seen! I don't know what it said to others, but for me that plane had freedom written all over it."

The prisoner broke her fast too quickly, too excessively. It was the richest meal of her life—sky, clouds, ocean, freedom. She came down long before the plane did. By the time the stewardesses were taking orders for lunch—"smorgasbord, ach!"—she couldn't keep her eyes open. She crashed—with a headache and a stomach ache. She slept cuddled up in a chair; she had never slept that way before. Ted's arm was around her: they had fallen asleep watching television and she had to get him up and on his way before her father . . . She heard the engines stop. She woke—in Ted's arms—with a headache and her period. They were on the ground—in Amsterdam!

She expected wooden shoes. Ted advised her to be patient until they got out of the airport. She tried, but she was in a foreign country! Her father and mother had never been there. Most of the people she knew had never been there. She was there! . . .

With a headache from home. They rode cobblestone streets to their hotel, which was on a canal. Through the throbbing in her eyes, she took inventory of their room: wooden-beam ceiling, brick walls, fireplace, old-fashioned curtains, lots of brass and glass. She would be fine; only right now she had to lie down, to sleep. Ted went to get tea, anything that might make her more comfortable. This was the first time she had been sick since they were married, and she wondered if he was already asking himself, Who needs this?

She felt better that night. It was time to see a little of Amsterdam. Perhaps it should have begun with the wooden shoes or the windmills, but several doors from the hotel was the house that Anne Frank had lived in and hidden in and been plucked from. As she crossed the inside doorway that had concealed the girl, Angela felt that she had known her, had shared something with her, discovered—as her heart pounded the way her head had earlier—a bond between prisoners, and another between herself and the only two people she knew who had escaped this, who had survived.

The next day began like a honeymoon. Amsterdam was casual, but Angela dressed for it. She was like a kid in an arcade. She didn't know what to take in first. They walked up and down "thissa strasse and thatta strasse." Bought little windmills and little shoes and little chocolates. And postcards.

That night, wide-eyed, she rode through the red-light district; red-faced, she sat at a local strip show. "And stared! It had nude men and women! It was some kind of ballet, very tastefully done . . . I think. . . . But I had never seen anything like it! So I just stared!"

They stayed very late. She felt very grown up and just like a kid at the same time. Ted was showing her the world now. "There were other things besides family! I had never thought of that before."

Before they left Amsterdam, Angela had her blood tested at the hospital. Dowling had insisted on a blood test in each country, with the results forwarded to him. By her.

"He still wasn't letting go. It wasn't a game anymore or even a contest, and I wasn't amused." Amsterdam, Brussels, Paris, Zurich, Rome: it took up a full day in each country—European hospitals were inefficient and dreadful—and Memorial had spoiled her. "It made me feel tied down and sickly. Here I was in Europe. I had all this freedom and I was throwing it all over the place, using it in every which way I possibly could, and Dowling had found a way, where my parents and Ted's parents and every other person in the world had failed, of limiting it."

*I*t was like the Bible, with all its "begats." Ted tried to explain it to her on the plane to Paris: Daniel was the son of Lillian's sister Deborah, who begat . . .

She liked having acquired cousins named Michel and Hélène and Daniel. And Daniel's wife, Danielle! She loved that—Danielle and Daniel. She asked Ted if he would change his name to Angelo—not very French, but that was the closest she could come. *"Pour moi?"*

Michel and Hélène were brother and sister, who couldn't do enough for them. They shared their home and their city with them. But Daniel did even more. He shared something deep inside himself, something Angela felt the moment she met him. Something with so much force that when she and Ted complained because he wouldn't let them take a franc out

120

of their pockets, making it impossible for them to reciprocate, Daniel would hug her, or both of them, grin proudly at Ted while mumbling something in "French-Yiddish" about Ted's mother, and make it strangely all right.

On the last of their eight nights in Paris, they sought Hélène's cooperation in making the evening theirs—financially. Hélène refused with the same enigmatic disclaimer they had heard several times before—"We are here to serve you"—and before they could pursue it, Michel admonished them once again to enjoy, please to enjoy. It was their next words to Angela, almost in unison, that sprang the trap: "Your mother-in-law is a wonderful woman!" Angela had forgiven her in-laws for much, but she hadn't quite got around to thinking that loftily about either of them (yet! she added with hope in her heart), nor had their own son, she surmised. "Why do you say that?" she asked. "You don't even know her!" And in a few words, surprisingly few, Hélène recited what she assumed they had already known.

"Daniel saw his mother drag away by Nazis, forever. Lillian save him. He was eleven ... her sister's son. ... She is mother for him. In concentration camp ... after concentration camp ... she always keep him alive."

Hélène stopped, and with no more words to focus on, no more accent to struggle with, Angela began to cry, freely, as she had tried never to let herself cry over anything concerning her in-laws, no matter how much they had hurt her, in their presence or otherwise. Her tears were unshared. In this other part of the world, even in this country characterized by intense responses, Michel and Hélène understood that in such a situation you don't show your emotions. And in spite of the turmoil inside him, Ted demonstrated his conditioning.

Daniel paid for the evening. Not a word was said about the conversation before dinner, at least not in English.

At the airport, he said to her, "We're both very lucky!" and she kissed him and said, "You're right!"

*S*he had had her picture taken in front of every major museum and cathedral—and her blood taken in practically every metropolitan hospital—in Europe. In the Vatican, at last, she practically volunteered to die: God, if you're going to take me, why not do it now? They had been away three weeks. They had planned four. She called home.

"Mom, I'm in Rome!"

"You're home?"

"No, I'm in Rome . . . Rome!"

"You're home, my baby, when did you get home?"

"I'm not home yet! RRROME! I'm in ROME!"

"Oh, I thought you were home. . . . It's been so long. . . . "

"I know, Mom, but I'll be home soon. Don't worry about anything."

It was time to go home. That night she told Ted. "There's only so much vacation we can take. The next sight I want to see is my own dirty dishes. I want to cook and I want to clean. I want to be a housewife. It may not be the most exciting thing in the world, but it is mine!—and I want to experience it. You can take a picture of me at our front door, over the stove, cleaning our toilet bowl. Let's get on the next plane!"

They sang "Arivederci, Roma" at the airport. They exchanged cozy thoughts on the plane. They were confident when they landed. Still, the photograph, slightly out of focus, shows him looking tan and her looking tired. Her mother almost ruined it in her hurry to get it over with, pull her daughter aside, and ask what was wrong. Her family came prepared to pick up where they had left off. They began to baby her.

If the young couple had thought about anything after the honeymoon . . . But they weren't prepared. They couldn't insist that her parents let them do things their way, because they didn't have a way in mind. Angela wasn't even aware that there was a problem. She had her own apartment, she had a husband she was sleeping and laughing with, and she could stay out as late as she wanted. That was marriage. She continued to ask her family what to do, and to do as they said. She was so sure they had all the answers for her that she hadn't thought for one minute about a future not decided by them after she put the ring on her finger.

Ted thought about it when the Ambrosias met them at the airport. When Mama carried Angela's flight bag for her. When she wiped her daughter's brow in the car. Ted thought about it every time the phone rang, which was too often ... always for Angela. Mom, Dad, or Camille.

They swallowed them up. Camille would call Dowling to discuss her state of health. Papa would ask Ted to put Angela on the phone so he could find out how she was feeling. Ted couldn't get cough medicine for her without Mom asking him if he had checked with Dowling first.

His "love and honor" were never in question, but no one was giving him the chance "to ... protect, till death do you part." Nor was he giving himself the chance. Or taking the chance. To Angela, he seemed stunned, frozen by this life-and-death situation he had got himself into. She discovered that while she was totally prepared to spend the rest of her life with him, she didn't have that much faith in putting it in his hands.

They were fighting—frequently—and she didn't understand why. They quickly got around to dragging both families into it, and she complained, "Your family doesn't care about me. No one calls. . . . " He didn't deny it or defend them; he just interrupted her with "Your family doesn't care about you either." Thinking twice about throwing that first something at him, she asked, at the top of her voice, how he could even say such a thing about her family and think that it would stick. He told her. "Because if they really cared about you, they'd leave you alone. They'd let us grow together and let us experience things for ourselves. But they're too involved. They care about you so much and they love you so much that it is consuming everything in sight; it's becoming a monster. They don't understand. They don't care about you as a person. They don't know you as a person. They just know about Angela, sick girl, whom they have to take care of and whom they love."

It hit home. She started to realize that something was wrong in her life. Not her life in the shadow of death, but her life to be lived. Maybe her people *were* doing something wrong. It was the first time she had ever thought of them that way.

At her mother's, several days later, when her mother heard Angela's new ideas—when her mother heard that she had such ideas of her own—she flew into a rage. When Ted tried to explain that Angela had to stand on her own two feet, her mother stood up from the table on *her* two feet and challenged both of them. "No one loves Angela more than I love her; no one cares for her more than I care for her." And Ted said, "You're wrong. . . . I do," and Mama said, "You can't," and it became a contest with both contestants appealing to the prize, Angela, for a decision. She was very confused, and being torn in two. Her body rebelled; she started to shake and couldn't stop shaking, and her mother said, "See what you've done . . . you've made her shake!" And Angela shook herself to her feet and screamed, "It's not him, it's you. It's you!"

If she had ever seen a barroom brawl, which of course she hadn't, she would have known that what followed was as close to one as mother and daughter could come. They screamed at each other, screamed over each other's voices, ignored Ted, who tried to

125

restrain them, who actually held Angela's arms back at one point, until they had screamed themselves out. Then they sat. Angela spoke first. "Why won't you let me grow up? Let me be a woman like you. Let me make a few mistakes." Silence. "Let us live our own lives. It's time you started accepting Ted as a man. Because if you don't, I never will." No answer. No disagreement, but no commitment.

Angela went to Dowling, as she always had when she had problems with her family. Perhaps she shouldn't have, because of Ted. But she and Dowling were getting along better now than they had for a long time, and once again he was the oracle for her. But the oracle sided with her family. For the first time. He didn't want to discuss her "case" with "anyone new." Any member of her family could, and did, call him at any time about any matter concerning her, no matter how inconsequential. But he wasn't available to her husband.

She stood on the street looking at the hospital she had walked out of so many times and never before looked back on. She had expected marriage to change everything. Somehow her leukemia would disappear forever and all her troubles fade away. Secretly, she hoped it might even be magical enough for her to have a child . . . maybe, someday. But it was no good; she felt so frustrated. Suddenly her relationship with Dowling didn't look so good again. She got angry, indignantly angry. She was going to go back in there, right back to Dowling, to have a showdown, to defend her husband, but—she couldn't. She couldn't risk Dowling. She couldn't sacrifice him. It was going to be harder than ever to go home now and put all her trust in Ted. Ted was right for the *fantasy* of marriage. But Dowling was always there, ready to handle the realities of everything else.

Just when she believed things couldn't get worse, Ted's family re-entered. Angela learned to laugh and cry at the same time. When she and Ted needed each other the most, his parents needed him. For the most trivial errands—couldn't he spare a little time for them? When she and Ted could withstand criticism the least, they were harshly criticized. Their marriage wasn't working; her in-laws wanted to know why she wasn't working. She was having trouble holding down her food—they wanted her to hold down a job.

She got a job as a dental assistant. Her husband was unhappy because he couldn't make her parents happy; maybe, if she could make her husband's parents happy, she could make him happy! But work didn't work either. He complained because she was so tired at night, and they contended that she shouldn't be tired when he came home after working so hard. Angela was the only one who actually got any pleasure out of it. She didn't do very much, but she loved getting out of the house every day. And she loved learning anything that Dowling might not know, and working it into their conversation on her next visit. But again she was criticized—for being away from home too much! She recalled, with laughter and in tears, when she had complained that the Rubels never called, and longed for the good old days of six or seven weeks ago. Thinking in her latest vocabulary, she concluded that she needed Ted's family like she needed a toothache, which—with God, like everybody else, on their side, it seemed to her—she got.

Angela, the "hotshot dental assistant," was hospitalized with four impacted wisdom teeth. This was the first crisis she and Ted were to face together. Her irregular platelet count, when low, created a condition similar to hemophilia. Any infection or operation was a threat to her health. She also considered any separation between her and her husband, at this time, another blow to their unsettled relationship. They had so many problems to solve and they weren't going to be solved in the hospital, with Dowling overseeing her, with familiar nurses greeting her, and everything around her suggesting that she was welcome there and that, even with a marriage license, her own toaster, and a double bed, she still had no permanent home of her own.

She lay in her hospital bed with her scale model of a set of teeth on the table next to her. She had painted the four wisdom teeth red with nail polish. She stared and stared at those teeth as if there were something to be learned from them. It was the first time in her medical life that she completely understood what was the matter with her and what was going to be done about it.

The teeth were extracted without complication. Her interest in dentistry disappeared just as fast, and with as little fuss. Their marital problems were temporarily anesthetized—she was relieved that in her absence Ted hadn't moved another woman in to cook and sew for him—but soon after her return home the numbness wore off and they were at it again. Coaxed from both corners.

She used to think: This can't be love, but if I didn't love him I'd give it all up. She used to think: Why didn't I marry Dowling and make everybody else happy—my family would stop worrying about me, Ted's family would stop bothering me, and I'd have some peace. She thought: If this is what I'm thinking, imagine what he's thinking!

"Saved by the flu!" Right back into the hospital. It was the first of four times she was hospitalized with flu that winter. Flu made her white count skyrocket and Dowling didn't know if it would come down. But Ted knew—he said it would. He told her it would and he told her family it would, and he was right! Until now, the world had been divided between Dowling on "the inside" and the two families "outside." But the hospital was Ted's turf, too—he had just proved it, and he'd been strong!—and it was Angela's, too. And she thought: Why can't we make the world outside ours, too?

*T*hey lived on the second floor of a two-family house adjoined by another two-family house. Five blocks from the house she was raised in, a mile from his, in Brooklyn. The three families around them had heard them at their worst, but they liked the brave young couple and never took sides, not even among themselves. They noted that the outbursts were fewer now, and tranquility followed faster.

She was home most of the winter, alone most of the day. She had furnished the apartment comfortably and was proud of it. But it was too large for her—a den she couldn't fill and a front porch she couldn't use. Most days the building was empty of people except for her. The telephone was company. It rang once and she answered, but the caller hung up. She'd had an obscene call several days previously—language she'd never heard before. She was sure she hadn't heard right, and said, "What?" and the caller repeated himself. Now her phone rang again, and again there was no one there. She was a little uneasy. She didn't want to wait for another phone call. She called Camille, mainly for the sound of her voice, and said very little, just listened. She thought she heard a sound from the downstairs hallway. Camille, already concerned about her sister's unaccustomed reserve, had asked several times if she was all right. When Angela heard another sound, she mentioned it as casually as possible to Camille, who became alarmed; then Angela talked herself—and Camille—out of it, blaming it on her imagination. She concluded with a promise to her sister that she would call her back if she heard anything else. She called the apartment downstairs and there was no answer. She went to her front door and opened it slightly, closed it tightly, locked it, and bolted it, and went right back to the phone. "Camille, I think I hear men's voices. Should I call the police?" "Yes, the police. I'll call Philip and you call the po—" and the line went dead. Angela thought: They're going to kill me! And then she thought: Oh, no, they're not. I didn't fight for my life for five years to die this way. Maybe "It's always something else that gets you," but it isn't going to be this! She fetched a Winchester rifle they kept on hand—unloaded: she was afraid of bullets—and paced, marched like a soldier. Heard something being dragged. Announced: "Ted, take the gun and go downstairs and blow their brains out!" Continued to carry on an imaginary dialogue. No more noises, not for a while, and that frightened her more. They were coming for her—stealthily. She put on a heavy coat, wrapped herself in another, and, although it was a warm day, put on boots to protect her feet when she jumped. She was going to hurl herself off the porch. When she looked down, she saw Philip, who demanded, over and over, "Where are they, where are they," and without waiting for an answer, "I'm coming in!" She ran in to get the keys for him, heard a crashing at the downstairs door, ran back to the balcony yelling, "Don't come in, Philip," ran back for the keys, heard the pounding on the stairs, heard it getting closer and thought they were chasing Philip, grabbed the rifle as her door broke open and Philip burst in, grabbed the rifle from her, instructed his German shepherd, Junior, to "get 'em, boy," and ran from room to room still asking, "Where are they, where are they?," still not listening to her, until he heard her say that there were no bullets in the gun, at which point he turned it upside down, began slashing the air with it, thrust Junior into the bedroom

131

with his instructions, and closed the door. They listened in awe to Junior's performance. Junior got 'em, all right—the drapes, the bedspread, and a large stuffed doll, which he mutilated. Philip calmed down enough to comprehend that her apartment had been invaded only by a few sounds. Breathlessly, "Camille said rape and murder and lines cut. .... C'mon, you shouldn't be here alone. I'm taking you to Mom's for the rest of the day. And you and your hysterical sister stay off the phone with each other from now on!"

She unwrapped herself, put on shoes, closed the broken door as best she could, and they descended. As they stepped outside, big brother coddling her, a pistol went to his head from behind and he was instructed to release the girl slowly and not to make another move or else. Suddenly the street was full of policemen; they closed in from every direction. Junior began to growl and Philip began to sweat. So his sister had been right, after all—there was an intruder. Angela was catatonic. A bullhorn began blasting: "Do not move! Do not move! We will shoot to kill!" No one was moving.

Mrs. Ambrosia, who had run the five blocks from her house to her daughter's, entered the street with those words ringing in her ears and ran toward the scene shouting, "Don't shoot, don't shoot, they're my children!" The voice on the other end of the pistol at Philip's head began talking to the police, who were surrounding him. And they talked back to him. In friendly terms! So his sister had been wrong—there was no intruder! It was another policeman. He,

132

Philip, was the intruder. One of the next-door neighbors, a little elderly lady, insinuated herself between the policemen and started hitting Philip over the head with her handbag, crying, "Animal, animal, what did you do to this wonderful girl!" With the gun still at his head, Philip ignored the blows of the stranger as he looked out of the corners of his eyes at the woman with the heaving chest throwing tranquilizers into her mouth, and stiffly implored, "Mom, please don't make a move! Please, Mom, don't make a move!"

One of the officers in charge had had enough and instructed several others to remove the two interfering women. As they seized Mrs. Ambrosia, Angela found speech again. "What are you doing to my mother?" "Your mother, I thought she was *his* mother!" And she explained, or tried to. The Ambrosias were frightened, everyone was confused and nervous. Asked for identification and verification of the relationship, Mrs. Ambrosia rummaged wildly through her purse, opened a packet, and poured the contents into the astonished man's hand. It was Angela's four wisdom teeth.

No one had bothered to call Ted.

*T*he news was full of Lisa Klinglesmith. She was famous at three. Dailies detailed the joy of a second successful liver transplant at Memorial. Television sets beamed with the bouncing child. In 1973, she was December's favorite continuing serial.

Angela followed with special fascination, in awe of such courage, confounded by one so young who could go through such hell and come out of it so alive. She had never seen herself that way.

It was Thursday, Angela's day for visiting the hospital as an outpatient. Dowling; then Ted. Sometimes lunch, if she hung around. Today she could be useful. She didn't recognize the child with the media smile, because Lisa was crying. She wasn't in pain. She wasn't even frightened. She was just being a child who'd run out of big-people patience. And Angela responded as she always did when she saw a distressed child. Like one of two intimate classmates swapping sandwich halves, she eased the little girl's anger with the love she'd brought from home. The results were so winning that she couldn't refuse the invitation of grateful parents to continue the remedy through the halls, in the elevator, and on into their daughter's room. There the little girl learned and repeated with delight the name of her new friend, Angela. And Angela was introduced to Mr., Mrs., and Lisa Klinglesmith.

Lisa was the color of a pink orchid and the size of a pillow. She had wavy honey-blond hair and round, large blue eyes. High cheekbones, pug nose, and a tiny red mouth. So far, so beautiful. But her face, naturally round, was bloated from medication; her little girl's figure was distorted by a potbelly large enough to make her look "like a midget in her seventh month of pregnancy." Her little stomach had been pumped with air for many days prior to the transplant to make room for the liver of a thir-teen-year-old boy.

Lisa entered Angela's life as a young friend in need when Angela needed to be needed. It got her out of the house again. She would travel from Brooklyn to Manhattan every day to visit her, comfort or amuse her. She became the child Angela couldn't have, the child Angela could prove she *should* have. Lisa refused to eat: Angela fed her, got her to eat—eventually, for anyone. She had forgotten how to walk: Angela, who'd been through this, worked with her, walked with her. She was afraid to complain: Angela listened, and the child unburdened herself. She became the child who would save Angela's mar-riage. Angela expected Ted to be as involved as she was. At lunch, she discussed Lisa with him as if they had vital decisions to make. They no longer discussed themselves. Lisa became Angela's obsession. Home at night, separated from her "child," worrying un-ceasingly, Angela prayed for her, prayed so hard, concentrated so intensely, that she would stop only when the inevitable headache made further devotion impossible. Ted forbore, gently counseled temper-ance, but Angela prevailed. It was not too great a sacrifice for *her* child.

While Lisa was still in the news, Angela almost became news herself. It had never occurred to her that she might have caused headlines, and if it had, the family-imposed secrecy surrounding her case would have explained it away. But a newscaster from a crew visiting Lisa wanted to know who she was, this young lady who had burst into the room bringing such sunshine with her and such light to Lisa's eyes. He recognized a good story and asked if he could use it. Just as Lisa would have done, Angela said she'd have to ask permission.

Dowling said no. She would have liked to be on television. She would have liked the world to know that she was special, too. She would have liked her in-laws to know, and her cousins. But Dowling said no, in the name of saving lives. He would be hounded, he said, unable to do his work. More time was needed for research, for more tests, more evidence, before they could remove the need for caution, before they could tell the world about the success he had had with Angela.

The cameras stayed on Lisa, even when she developed unphotogenic sores on her tender scalp as a result of a staphylococcus infection. Her doctor explained to the audience that her antibodies were low because of the immunosuppressive drugs they had given her for the past six months so that her body would not reject the new liver; he declared a moratorium on cameras. So that they could reduce her pain with morphine, which he didn't explain. As much morphine as they would give an adult, which he didn't mention. When Angela visited her, Lisa could barely open her eyes, and a hello, even a smile from her, was impossible. For goodbye, for tangible contact, Angela put her index finger—the one she would have wagged at her, and said, "You get better now!"—in the limp little hand. And there it was: those soft hands, soft like tissue paper, and damp; so

136

soft they felt as if you could put your finger through them; the hands of Annie, of others. Heartbreakingly familiar: the hands of death.

Angela moved closer to Lisa only a few days later—she was admitted to the hospital with an inflamed throat and swollen glands—but in spite of her proximity to her beloved friend, two floors away, she could not come near her for fear of giving her the flu. She inquired about Lisa, sent her messages, and listened to the radio for "the truth." Her own stay, brief but difficult, had left her severely debilitated, and five days later, when she went home, it was her family's home she went to; she couldn't be left alone, and Ted had to agree that until she was fully recovered the only place for her was with her mother.

She spent most of the first three days in the basement recreation room. She put her hands together to pray and tried not to think about Lisa's hands, unless she could think them firmer, drier. She listened for news: TV was silent on the subject; a kind voice on the radio had spoken with confidence for a while, then said nothing. Her mother came and went without commenting on the obvious, and Angela said nothing, not wanting her to interfere. She was alone when Ted called to tell her that Lisa was dead. She screamed and Mama came running.

Lisa had died of a staph infection. That was all. Angela felt as if everything had been torn out of her. In the hollow, she heard: "It's always something else that gets you." In the emptiness, she trembled.

When the sound of her mother's voice reached her, she managed, "Lisa is dead," and she shook with tears. "Is that all? You scared the daylights out of me! I thought Dowling had given you bad news! She's not even related to you. What did you have to get involved for? Why did you have to get hurt?" Her mother fought back her own tears. "Get up on your feet and stop feeling sorry for everybody else and start taking care of yourself! I won't have you carrying on like this over strangers!"

Angela kept saying, or thought she was saying, "How can you say that! How can you say that!" She felt her lips moving, saw her mother's lips moving long after they had ceased to make sense. It was the first time in her life she had ever been ashamed of her mother.

She had to get out of that house. She flew, like a rush of air, like the cyclone from that TV commercial, up the stairs and out the front door. Without thought, without consideration for the rain and the cold and her health, she headed for the church.

She pounded on the thick doors that wouldn't admit her and yelled, "Let me in, let me in," but all she heard in the dark echo was "involved, involved. . . . " She ran next door to the priests' home and found Father Ritchie, who put a coat and a supporting arm around her and took her back to the church, where they prayed together, and then talked. First about the child; then about the mother, both mothers. And he seemed so sure that Mrs. Ambrosia had been protecting her daughter. "She was lashing out at this baby that had hurt you, her baby. She doesn't want you to suffer any more, and she didn't want you to suffer . . . helplessly . . . for someone else—this child. She knows what that's like. You'll always be her baby."

Angela understood, but she couldn't go back there. She understood more now. Her mother would be furious with her for having gone out in the rain— she was still her baby. She had made a mistake returning there to convalesce—she still hadn't moved out. It always seemed to take a shock for her to learn anything . . . she'd have to work on that . . . but right now—she didn't want to be theirs anymore! She was going home—to Ted. She walked.

Ted said: "You're twenty-one and a half. Do you realize that you've never been on a bus or taken a train by yourself? That you've never gone for a walk alone? That up until tonight you were afraid of getting lost in your own neighborhood!"

She asked her family to give them six months. She meant: give Ted six months. Six months to prove himself. She was negotiating for her independence.

"If he can't take care of my life . . . if he can't live up to the standards I need him to live up to, then I'll leave him. . . . "

She asked herself if she meant it. It sounded hard. She felt the need to clarify it a little—for herself— for her self-image.

"My welfare has to be on top in this relationship.

Not because I want it that way, but because it has to be that way. Ted and I both know that. He has to be there for me. He has to be a superman of men when it comes to my being ill—the one I want to go to . . . the one I want to believe."

It was done.

Six uneventful months. She stayed healthy, worried only occasionally and secretly about the next six months. He encouraged her, thought about the future. In shared respect they found shelter, and settled in. His family was quietly vindictive; hers, vindictively quiet.

"I thought I would die at twenty-two, because that's how old Eric was when he died. It haunted me. If I could just hang in there to twenty-three . . . "

Her birthdays were a big deal to her family— each one after her sixteenth was a miracle. They would all gather and give thanks, congratulate themselves, and, in what became a traditional closing ritual, stand facing north and thumb their noses in the direction of—*at*—Memorial Hospital. Thanks for another year.

She didn't make a fuss over her approaching birthday. Nor, when the time came, would she let Ted or anyone else, and it came and went quietly. Two weeks afterward, she was taken, in pain, to the hospital. She didn't have flu and she didn't have a blood clot.

"She's not sick," insisted her mother.

"But her white count is soaring ... her platelets ... the Philadelphia chromosome again ... the tests ... "

At sixteen, Angela thought her mother was ashamed of her. At twenty-two, Angela understood that her mother was still trying to protect her. Still overprotecting her, as Ted pointed out, by phone from Boston, where he was hopelessly trapped on hospital business. "Just when it looked like we had finally won permanent custody of me!" Angela said, *after* she and Ted hung up. They took her home with them. The jury reconvened. For the next few days she was theirs again.

It was hushed-voice time in the living room once more. While the women bit their lips, the men their fingertips, Camille, and then Tony, and then—Mom—broke the terrible news to her. The leukemia was back. Her stomach turned over a few times and she thought: So I wasn't cured, after all. As in her childhood when her parents had reneged on a promise to take her somewhere, she was disappointed. Disappointed enough to cry. And poor Dowling—he was so proud; how was he going to take this? And Ted—he was supposed to be with her now! What had she got him into!

Her jury had just sentenced her to death. They

were frightened, waiting for her reaction. Whatever it was they were braced for, they weren't going to get it from her.

"All right," as she rose and went around the room with her right hand extended, palm up and open, "give me all the money you have on you. Every penny," she prodded—and waited for. "If I'm going out, I'm going out in style." The essence of style, to someone who had dressed through most of her teens for a hospital bed, was still nightgowns. That afternoon, she and Camille went shopping. The next morning, Angela entered the hospital in high machine-washable style.

It was all a front—the style, the humor, the guts. It dissolved as they prepped her at the hospital. Her brain had reacted with dignity, behaved obediently, even if peculiarly; but her body was catching up to it—irrational about chemotherapy and atheistic about a second miracle. "Why is she shaking so?" asked a nurse who had to be very new to the hospital not to know the patient, not to know why. A shotgun answer came from a young resident, so full of sympathy for Angela he had none left for the novice: "Shut up!"

They gave her Demerol to stop the shaking. It slowed her down . . . way down. They started her on intensive chemotherapy immediately. She responded traumatically, regurgitated violently. She took to the Compazine they prescribed for the nausea, plus the codeine shots and the Darvon they administered, as if she were on speed.

As she sped up, she heated up. Her temperature

climbed to a whistling one hundred and six. They
called for an ice blanket. She was stripped naked and
laid, like a corpse, face up, head to toe on a pad connected to an electric socket. She tensed, expecting a
chill, but as it heated up she thought: This isn't so
bad. Then they unplugged it, hoisted her up, and sent
for the right pad. It was worse than she had
expected—an upholstered bed of ice on which she lay
sweating and shivering, skin and scars irradiant,
while interns and others shuffled in and out of the
room all night.

By morning, her lips were violet, her tears formed
mini-stalactites around her ears, and her temperature was still a hundred and six. They lifted her,
lowered her, and bathed her. She levitated. At least
twice, nurses commented on how soft her skin was.
Soft and moist . . . clammy, she recalled, and wondered: Is this it?

She wore two nightgowns and waited. The night
nurse, or "she-who-stuck-by-night," filled her with
sedatives. The day nurse said she wasn't getting
enough sleep and looked yellow. Angela told her it
was the hospital lighting . . . told her it was her olive
Italian complexion . . . told her to get Dowling and to
hurry, please! She was out of condition for being this
sick or this frightened. She couldn't bear it anymore.

Dowling gave her his once-over look—he obviously wasn't going to alter his bedside manner to suit
her marital status—and she was with an old friend
and felt a little relieved already. "You saw it coming,
didn't you?" That explained why he had said no to her
about the publicity and the cameras: he had used

143

himself as an excuse. The nurse repeated that Angela looked yellow. Dowling said that perhaps she looked terrible, but her skin looked fine, and started comparing Angela's arm to his. "See, she's the same color as me."

"But you're yellow," Angela practically sang. "Your skin has always been a little yellow." She laughed and coughed and thought the joke was on him. But as always, she reckoned moments later, it was on her. She had jaundice.

Always ready and willing to understand, she understood. Her body could no longer contain all the poison inside it, so it had to come out through the skin. She felt exposed. And guilty. She lifted the shoulders of her gown. Somehow she had sinned but, like everything else, it could be treated. She smiled and said she'd be fine. She wanted Ted.

Alone, she could have cried. No, she couldn't; she could have laughed—until her insides burst, until she turned purple and yellow. But it would have hurt her throat too much. Instead of stifled laughter, what the doctor on night rounds found "by the light of his silvery laryngoscope" was tonsillitis.

Next to the chemo bottles and the plasma bottle and the dextrose bottle on her i.v. pole, they hung the penicillin. The rest of the remedy wasn't so funny either: she was handed a suppository. "Oh, no," she rasped, "I'm not putting this up . . . " "You don't have to," the intern said. "We want you to suck on it." She could tell he was serious—perverted, maybe, but serious. "Oh, that makes me feel much better! Is this Halloween candy?" He finally convinced her—by

144

crossing his heart—that other patients had taken them, that it was the best way of maintaining prolonged action in the throat. She unwrapped it—paused while the degradation passed—and tried it. He threw a few more on her bed table, ran "often as possible" and "good girl" together, and left. There are no taste buds where suppositories are made to go. It was worse than medicine.

"My wise-guy brother-in-law, Tony, kidded me that my tongue would probably turn black. It did. From the penicillin!" Every few hours for several days, she had to stick it way out while someone scraped it and swabbed it. It felt like a cow's tongue and it hurt. She had no taste whatsoever. "Naturally, I was off the suppositories by then."

Ted had returned sometime "between the yellow skin and the black tongue." He was with her as much as possible, and having him with her always made her feel a little bit better somewhere. But she ached everywhere. She was living on pain-killers and Ted knew it and couldn't stop it. She was embarrassed that he knew, but she couldn't stop it—living on them—either. She managed to coax them out of everybody in the hospital, and when she couldn't get what she wanted she got hysterical. She became addicted to Darvon, about a hundred a week, plus the Demerol. Without the Darvon, she became nauseated, hot and dizzy, tired, anxious and hyper. And mean! She cursed Dowling, and cursed at him, for not letting her have more. And paranoid! She accused Ted of swiping what they gave her. She even tried to leave the hospital once, because she had some at home and she was that desperate. With the pills—only with them—Angela felt normal.

She got thinner and thinner. She had abdominal pain and she was constipated. And she was stoned. "I used to try to put things in my mouth and they would wind up in my ear."

Nevertheless, the chemo had to continue at all costs—to her. Her hair began to fall out, first from her body and then from her head. It was the first time Angela had ever lost her hair, and she hated herself. Then it ate a hole, about the size of the tip of her little finger, in her cheek. She couldn't escape herself: "No matter where I held on or hugged when my head spun wheels and my stomach ground gears, I was reminded of my ugliness." She decided that in spite of her mother, she was good and sick.

Her face became contorted with pain. Her bite was skewed by vincristine. Lips and one cheek were forced upward and cramped beneath her squinting right eye. So was the right shoulder, up and over the neck, joining her tilted head at the jawline, thereby leaving the crescent-shaped left side of the neck where symmetry was expected. She had to do an isometric in order to vomit.

They finally took her off the chemo—because they had to—and gave her something milder: her "latest pet wonder drug," hydroxyurea. The vomiting stopped. The headaches idled. Her eyes opened by themselves again. This she could manage. She felt herself getting lucky again.

"Ted was with me when my stomach caught fire." He tried to take charge, but was helpless to do anything for her. "Dowling, to the rescue, abruptly ordered Ted to take me down to his department and X-ray me—carefully, he added. As if he'd been careless with me. Ted's pictures showed that my wonder drug had burned my stomach to shreds. I became somebody's ulcer patient."

She had a new kind of headache. One that sawed her head in half, that blinded her. That made her irrational. That burned her nostrils and pinched her teeth. She huddled in agony, gnashed in frustration, screamed for Dowling, for Darvon, for help.

It began to appear that Angela was falling apart faster than they could put her together again. "I had been through hell before. I wasn't new to crisis. But this was the first time I had leukemia. For me! What a difference knowing that made. I was terminal. For the first time. Death wasn't an accident; living was. A happy accident! I was death-defying, and victory hinged on a happy accident."

It was the first time for Ted, as well. And for his family. It was the first time Angela's father-in-law saw her ill, and when he saw her in the hospital bed, white on white, the lesson of the past—you don't show your emotions; it's too dangerous—failed him, and he turned away and cried. She saw that.

Angela's case reached a point where Dowling began to feel incompetent. Afraid he was missing things. Haunted by the threat that she might convert to acute leukemia at any moment and he might miss it. Might lose her. He began sending other doctors to see her. Unable to find anything new to report, they diagnosed her symptoms in terms of her doctor

147

and her past—in terms of the unusually complicated doctor-patient relationship. What they knew about the case that didn't appear on her chart got directly in their way. The best they could do was attribute "these bizarre neurologic abnormalities" to a hysterical unwillingness on her part to give Dowling up. Dowling was impatient and incredulous: "Her feelings about me, past or present, are totally irrelevant. . . . Forget about them. Just go back and find out what's wrong with her!" They failed. As he thought he had failed. Either he and they were all medically incompetent in this case or—*or*—it dawned, exploded on him—they were right and her feelings about him weren't so irrelevant! That day which he would worry about some other day long into the future, after he had saved her—that problem which he thought had resolved itself when she got engaged—was here, was now, and he was simply failing to cope with it, not doing what she wanted him to do, whatever that was.

While every doctor asked her the same questions, and all the doctors asked the same ones over and over, Angela sank and continued to sink. Ted was having trouble keeping up with her, and if she couldn't hold on to him, there was nothing to keep her from going under. She began having convulsions. During one seizure, his family and hers, never easy with each other and caving in under the pressure, clashed, practically over her bed. Both sides agreed Ted shouldn't be involved. Angela tried to come to her husband's defense, and her own: in her delirium, she threatened Ted's irritating sister with "I am not in my right mind. Leave us alone or I am going to kill you." She doesn't remember. Nor does she remember inflicting a deep gash on her marriage by appealing to her brother-in-law: "Tony, please help me! Ted doesn't understand." He did and he didn't. He cried.

Dowling was direct. "We have to get you well enough to get out of here as soon as possible. You're crumbling emotionally and you're too young for that. You're not going to make it at this rate. I want you to see a psychiatrist."

In the middle of that night, or perhaps the night after, a light came through her window. "A pair of hands emerged from the light and passed over my body, just inches away, and then my head, taking the pain away with them as they disappeared. It wasn't a dream—I saw those hands. But I never saw such beautiful hands on a human being. They weren't attached to anything but the light."

Several days later, she was given "time off." Ted picked her up and they walked out of the hospital in silence, frightened of what was to come next for the two of them.

*D*r. Downs, the psychiatrist, had carpeting in his halls, outside his apartment! Angela had never seen that before. She was impressed. It gave her as much confidence in him as his fee did. For fifty dollars an hour and carpeting outside the apartment, she knew she was getting the best.

For his first fifty dollars, the psychiatrist told her

that she was a spoiled child. She hated him, but she returned with another fifty. He told her again; also that she had no identity of her own. She thought he was crazy. He asked to see her credit cards, her driver's license, her checkbook, her Social Security number. She couldn't produce any of them. He had made his point.

She and Ted were fighting with more anger than ever. About anything and everything. They couldn't even agree on what they were fighting about. If she blamed the chemo for wrenching her guts up, he blamed the psychiatrist for wringing her brain out. Dr. Downs, fostering her ego, told her she had two basic choices: stay, and face all her problems, or leave. "It was easier for me to think of leaving Ted than to begin to straighten everything out, to let everyone know just where Angela Rubel was at. Ted wasn't helping. He didn't want to hear what Dr. Downs had to say—not when it went against him— and he refused to meet with him, as the doctor had requested. I started thinking: Maybe I don't love him that much. He's got problems besides me. That he doesn't want to solve. I've got enough problems all my own. I need to worry now about that schmuck!"

His parents always needed him when she needed him, and she needed him more. A Rubel problem was always a bill or an errand, and they had four other children. But she was in pain and he worked in a hospital—why couldn't he supply her with as much Darvon as she needed? No, she wasn't going to kill herself, she screamed into the phone or into his face, although it wasn't such a bad idea!

She hounded him about the Darvon. She took as much as she could get her hands on. She slept most of the day; it was better than getting up and facing her problems. When she wasn't thinking about Darvon, or what to do about his family or her own family, who were back in the picture, she thought about death. She couldn't believe in herself as being able to live through the next few months. The more she tried not to feel sorry for herself, the more she thought about the blow she had been dealt and the sorrier she felt.

From her outpourings, Dr. Downs concluded that Ted was unable to cope. He was very good at handling small problems—his parents had trained him well for that—but he was unprepared to handle her big ones. His willingness to do every little deed that his family asked of him at such an inopportune time was his way of excusing himself, forgiving himself, for his deficiency.

She couldn't help herself. She began to despise him.

Ted was about to crack. He had to contend with his family, her family, Dowling, her, her Darvon addiction, her medical bills, the uncertainty of having her—in sickness or in health—for much longer, and now her psychiatrist.

To defend himself—against her or her psychiatrist—he agreed to see him, and admitted it made a bit more sense when it came direct. And listened when he encouraged them to try and make a life for themselves again, at all costs. And thanked him.

Then Dowling gave her her usual prescription for the chemo and she refused it. Not today, she said; I

151

just don't feel like it today. She hadn't planned such a radical first step. "You can't afford to miss," he told her. "Your body does unpredictable things and there's no telling what it might do." She leaned forward in her chair. "Look at me, look at what I look like. I'm thin, I'm yellow. I don't have a hair on my damned head. I'm falling apart. My marriage is falling apart. Ted and I argue twenty-four hours a day, that's all we do is get on one another's nerves. We can't survive much longer." Leaning closer. "Can you tell me that if I take it for another six months, even a little longer, till I'm twenty-three, I'll be all right?" "Angela . . . you'll probably have to take this, somehow, for the rest of your life." A silence with a memory of other showdowns filled the room. Till he offered it again. "I have to discuss it with my husband," she said.

Ted knew she was doing it as much for him as for herself. "Are you sure you want to do this?" For them. He would face, with her, whatever the consequences were to be. "I love you, and don't want to lose you. . . . " But she was the one who did the vomiting and she was the one whose life was at stake. "I know it will be all right, Ted, I just know it. But I can't do it without your support." His first departure from small problems was not a large decision, but a monumental acquiescence.

"And so it was. We didn't know whether I would live or die. All we knew was that at last we were going to have some peace again in our home and the opportunity, however brief, to live the lives we wanted to. Our lives."

Dowling had warned Camille that something like this might happen—anytime, once she was married. If husband and wife stood together, then family and doctor be damned. The first time she tried to assert herself, she and Ted were rookies and were no match for the undefeated team that divided them and, abetted by a tackle from the sidelines—four fortuitous wisdom teeth—rolled over them. This time, however, she was seasoned, knew the moves, and he was standing firm beside her: "She wants it this way; she has every right to have it this way." Furthermore, if the rules couldn't be altered to accommodate them, they were prepared to forfeit the game. Aware once again that he could do nothing if she refused to do it, too, Dowling deferred.

" . . . And we decided," she told her family after the build-up, and they interrupted, "You don't decide anything. When there's a decision to be made, Dowling will decide!" Which meant "we'll decide," as well. Which meant everyone but Angela and Ted will decide, again. Not this time. They went over and over it, her family getting increasingly emotional and pulling out all the stops. But they weren't going to God-and-guilt her, either. Not this time.

Her mother-in-law walked right into her. By telephone, without even bothering to ask how she was feeling. "Angela, tell Ted he has to—" Angela didn't wait for more. She was learning—"from barracudas"—to pounce quickly. "Ted doesn't have to do anything but take care of me, and right now he's got his hands full doing that. I don't want you pestering him with silly things anymore. He's your son, and if you and your husband want to be a mother and father to him, you're welcome to him. But don't make this a contest. Because . . . I'll cut you off from him. I can do it."

She didn't have to. They both discovered that if their families couldn't have them the way they wanted them, they didn't want them. The Rubels moved just right of Righteousness; Mr. and Mrs. Ambrosia left for Florida, contending it was the only way they could "withdraw." The phone stopped ringing.

They started to like each other. They started to want each other again, for better and better and better.

Yet after such harmony, her head throbbed with one haunting counterpart, triplets, harsh alliterative triplets—twen-ty-two . . . twen-ty-two . . . —like a triple-tongued trumpet, "Carnival of Venice" without melody. *Death in*—twen-ty-two . . . twen-ty-two . . . She never sang it out loud and he never overheard it. If it would only sing twenty-three!

They made plans to move—part of another beginning. That they made plans at all was prophetic. He never treated her like a sick person. She began to cut back on the Darvon. She had good days and bad days; on bad days she contended. Still, because she *felt* them, they had good in them.

She called her mother and father, Camille and Tony, Philip and Johanna, "just to let you know we're all right." She wasn't ready to do that with Ted's family, but she encouraged him to do so if . . . "We're doing so well, Ange. We're falling in love with each

154

other again. Why go back to them right now and let them tear us apart!"

Angela started visiting the park and the playground. She wanted more life, wanted it all around her. She sat on benches, and she borrowed—people, dogs, birds, children. She would rock a baby carriage for any mother who wasn't afraid of her—she still had no hair, a grotesquery to some that her hats failed to conceal, and in spite of sunglasses she squinted terribly. She thought the sound of crying babies and barking dogs was beautiful; it drowned out the throbbing in her head. But she wanted to hold an infant in her arms, to feed one and burp one and change a diaper, and no one was going to permit "the ghoul of Gravesend" to do that. No one but family, perhaps.

Johanna and Angela had always been more like school friends to each other than sisters-in-law, so Johanna was the only one she thought of calling. Angela asked her if she and Philip were planning to have a baby soon. Johanna's answer was that they weren't planning to have a baby at all. Angela tried to talk her into it, told her she wouldn't have to do a thing, not a thing; she would take care of it for her. Johanna asked the obvious: what about the first nine months? Angela said, "Oh, please!" and then, because she never was able to hold back much from her, she told Johanna why it was so important to her, and they talked the rest of the evening about it. Philip gathered enough from Johanna's side of the conversation to get on the phone and tell his sister that she was crazy, that she had enough to do just to take care of herself. But Johanna understood. The next morning, when Philip wasn't around, she called to suggest that Angela talk to Fran, Ted's brother's wife, who already had three children—a girl of five, a girl of three, and an infant boy—and could probably use her help.

Fran was bowled over. And reluctant. Angela only wanted to take occasional care of her nephew, she said: for an hour, an hour a day, a day a week, a week—and my nieces—oh, please! An act of charity, as far as Angela was concerned—one she wasn't too proud to jump up and down with joy for—Fran began to share her children with her.

She couldn't understand why mothers complained—it was thrilling. She watched with envy while Fran listened to one child, kept an eye on another, and changed the little one. This was a family! Angela decided she wanted three children, too, then remembered that she couldn't have any. She proudly paraded "our brood" into the park, noted that boys were much rougher than girls, but told Fran that she favored little boys anyway and wanted her first one to be . . . She was doing it again.

"I can take care of them," Angela insisted. "Go take care of what you have to do." She practically pushed Fran out the door, and Fran returned too soon. The next time she begged her to take a little longer, and the time after that longer still. At night, Angela boasted to Ted how she'd had her hands full with the children.

Being a wise man, he bought her a dog.

She would have slept so well then. If only she

could have blocked out the nocturnal throbbing. She went to sleep with it and she woke up with it. And she woke up with it getting gradually louder. And suddenly, louder! The trumpets were earsplitting and the waves of dactyls cavernous. Twen-ty-two ... twen-ty-two ... The "t"s struck like a jackhammer. Her hands could barely hold her head together. She couldn't call Ted; she couldn't let go. Through the ringing and the barking, and the pounding, the pounding, she heard a child crying. Fran was at the door.

"Please"—she sucked in ... out ... in again—"Memorial!"

Fran called Johanna, who lived only two blocks away, to take the children. And the dog. However, instead of them getting out of Fran's car at Johanna's, Johanna, who was not herself, got in, only half dressed, and Fran efficiently sped away.

All the way to the hospital, the children looked with curiosity at their Aunt Angela, but no one asked her why she held her hands over her ears—it was absolutely quiet in the car—and no one asked her why she shook—it wasn't cold—and no one asked Johanna or Mother anything, either.

The doctor, a new one, took his time examining her. Fran and the children went with Ted, who also had to keep an eye on Josh, Angela's dog, panting in the car. Angela kept Johanna with her. She knew it wasn't leukemia; it couldn't be. But Angela was sure she knew what it was. Johanna held her hand—Angela gave it to her—while the doctor was out of the room. Whatever he had given her for the pain

157

was beginning to work, but she still couldn't put her head down; she was sitting up at the foot of the bed when he re-entered. He said she would have to stay in the hospital, and she backed into a corner, screaming. "You're not going to kill me! Not now! Not when I'm doing well! You're not going to kill me!" Johanna wrapped her arms around her and tried to get through. Angela had lived with it for years. She hadn't told Ted and she hadn't told the psychiatrist or Dowling or anyone. But she had been opened up again, and it poured out. "I'm gonna die, Johanna. I've got a brain tumor!" She wouldn't listen to Johanna or anyone. "Look at the facts—Eric had the same leukemia I do, the same protocol, the same exact everything . . . and he died at twenty-two. He warned me it's always something else that gets you—and he died of a brain tumor."

She stayed—for one night. They convinced her to stay so that they could prove she was wrong. She didn't let Ted do her scans, and she made him swear that no one would swap pictures on her. They stood in line to convince her—Ted, Dowling; they said you name it and she did. In the long run, it was Mr. Deeds, with those tender eyes that couldn't lie, who brought a smile to her face. The head pains, diminishing with each oath and disclaimer, ceased. Twenty-two became a number to play when she got to Las Vegas someday. She left, convinced.

"That Saturday I powdered the top of my little bald head and Tony took me shopping for a wig. It was 'look healthy, be healthy' therapy, and I guessed it was as exciting as choosing a prom dress. I lost my

158

hat on one of the counters—could someone have bought it?—and people stared a lot, but I didn't blame them; I smiled a lot; I might have stared, too. However, to one lady who stared and stared, disapprovingly, I, in my best Katharine Hepburn, declared, 'Madam, you are going to be fat and ugly for the rest of your life. I, on the other hand, am going to get my hair back and become beautiful again.' "

When Fran's baby saw her in a wig, he cried.

Remission isn't something one celebrates. It isn't cure; it isn't conclusive. It's respite, a pit stop, a stay of execution. It isn't good news, it's better news. No one celebrates better news.

They knew before she left the hospital. But they knew she wasn't in any state to accept too much from them. The irony was that it was more important to dispel her fears of a brain tumor. The good news— the better news—could wait several days.

It came undramatically. Dowling called. Then Ted called. The rest of the day stayed the same.

She was sitting in her new apartment the next day thinking about death—in a melancholy way— when the Leukemia Society returned her phone call. She was finally in a high-rise building, with a doorman and self-service elevators. In Riverdale—a solid hour from Brooklyn. What a shame it would be to have to leave this too soon, she thought.

She had called the Society the day before yesterday to offer herself as inspiration: she had leukemia, she wasn't on medication, and she was staying alive. She thought that information might be useful to somebody. She had guessed correctly, but now she had to apologize: she was in remission, she didn't have it anymore. To her own surprise—she felt like an emotional orphan at the moment—she was relieved when they said they wanted to meet her anyway.

She spent a week cramming for health. A little weight, a little color, lots of energy. What she couldn't put into her complexion she put on her back; she arrived at the Society's offices a vision of well-tailored peaches and cream—cream-colored suit, peach sweater, cream and peach and brown scarf. This time when people stared, and stared, they were supposed to. They couldn't believe she had ever been sick.

While she answered questions, the door she had gently opened an hour ago swung open wildly and the gentleman they had sent for, Robert Rolnik, Producer—that was how he was introduced, or announced—sailed in, his two thumbs and forefingers framing her for the camera while he gushed adjectives and indicated that his search for Scarlett O'Hara was at an end at last.

It was a fifteen-minute television film for the Leukemia Society. They had been trying for a year and a half to find their girl. Now they had her—their girl had always wanted to be the star of something. It wasn't exactly Hollywood, she realized, but shooting began next week.

She was supposed to meet Rolnik and crew on

location in Central Park. Ted drove her there on his way to work. They started early but couldn't find anybody, and it was getting late for both of them and tempers were flaring. He slammed on the brakes and cursed. She retaliated. "Go to work! Just leave me here, leave me in the middle of the Park!" And she saw a police car. She was out of the car and on her way to the patrol car for directions, and its two patrolmen were out of their car and on their way to her, when she noticed that they had their guns drawn, and one of them grabbed her and the other one was heading directly for Ted. And she was asking the questions: "What's going on? What did we do?" "Are you all right, lady?" And she tried to explain as the other one pinned Ted up against their car and frisked him, only she couldn't find the beginning in her mind. "We were having an argument. He's Ted. . . . My mother has the teeth. . . . " She heard herself say it, she couldn't believe it; she wanted to swallow it back, but the patrolman had heard it, too. He relaxed his hold on her. He took a careful look. "I thought you looked familiar. I moved to another borough to get away from nuts like you. Can't you stay out of trouble?" And, gesturing toward Ted, "Is this another brother?" While Ted, his face to the side of the car and the blue weight pressing on him, watched in baffled silence, the policeman put away his pistol and listened and shook his head from side to side as she clarified the situation. He waved his partner off Ted, promising to try to explain it to him later. "Let's just get outta here before the rest of the family shows up!"

161

Ted and Angela didn't move as the car pulled away: they hadn't moved before it reversed itself and returned. The loquacious one addressed Ted sympathetically: "You married into a crazy family." And to her: "C'mon, get in. Let your husband go save some lives. We'll find your moviemakers." Ted opened the back door of the patrol car for her, closed it, and watched in wonder as they sped away.

No one expected her to arrive with police escort. The siren was blaring, on the chance that if the policemen couldn't find the crew, the crew would find them. As she stepped out of the car, Dowling, who was also about to make his film début, was the first to greet her. "I don't believe it! This is the way you get around?" There are girls who would have been mortified. Not her. "Of course. I'm a star."

She was a guest on the Leukemia Radiothon. Celebrity-victim. She made her pitch. While she was on the air, Ted's five-year-old cousin died of leukemia. That evening, she got a call from the father of a dying young man. His son had been listening and, with the first hope he had ever held, believed she could cure him. The next day, she and Ted were scheduled to go to Florida for a much-needed rest for both, but that night she went to the hospital. The young man asked her to pray for him; she said she would pray *with* him—if he would get out of bed, which she had been informed he had not done since taking ill. They sat on chairs facing each other. He took her upraised hands in his and squeezed tightly, so tightly that she thought she might lose her breath. "Make me well, Angela. I want to live." It frightened her. "I can't heal, I can only pray for you." He began to cry. How do you let someone down whose life may depend on his faith in you? "But my prayers are very powerful. Pray with me." His parents were waiting outside the room. Not only had he not stirred from his bed, he hadn't combed his hair or held a full conversation with anyone in weeks, and he had done it all for her in an hour. Even if he died tomorrow, at least he had lived a little today. Amen. Would she see others?

They all thought she had the power to heal. At the least, it was her faith that could keep them going a few more hours. She was too drained to go anywhere the next day. Or the next. And the phone kept ringing. More requests for visits, more prayers, more expressions of gratitude. Always for children. She kept coming back, terrified of what she might be doing and conscience-stricken about what she might fail to do. She lost several of her congregation in those few days; with each one she was a little more diminished. Only a child of her own could ever, in any way, supplant such loss.

Ted was resolute—tomorrow they were leaving for Florida. Their unborn, unconceived child was the one child that could be kept waiting. Perhaps not for too long, if she really wanted it, he encouraged.

She had to tell somebody. She blurted the news to Dowling—Ted and I are thinking about a baby! Dowling was apoplectic. A baby! And ineffectual. Use your heads! Ted was summoned. A year ago, when she briefly suspected she had, through her own

163

negligence, become pregnant, Dowling, enraged, blamed him: "He's supposed to be a man! How stupid can he be?" Now Dowling would show him! Other doctors were summoned to convince her. Dowling would show both of them.

It was like a police interrogation. They threw the book at her: perpetrating a monster; aiding and abetting blood clots; illegal use of hormones; inciting white cells to riot. But they couldn't pin a thing on her—on cross-examination, they always ended with "We don't know for sure." One fact was certain—her failure to plead guilty established them as the injured parties: "If you do, it'll probably kill you. You're going to take all our work, all our success with you, and make it for nothing."

The next morning she was too unraveled to get on a plane. Ted packed the car, packed Angela, in a heap of exhaustion, into it, and drove south, eventually to Florida.

"*I* stopped taking precautions. I know what night it was. March 1, 1976. My twenty-fourth birthday."

They were staying with her parents in Port Richey, Florida. The four of them had done the usual nose-thumbing in the direction of Memorial, and all the rest. Then Angela and Ted excused themselves and went upstairs to bed. They had saved the best present ever for last. She removed the wrapping and they played awhile. Then, they got scared. They stopped and waited in the dark.

"Ted, do you think they're right?"

"I don't know, Ange. I wish I did."

"Do you want a child?"

"Yes, as much as you do, but I don't want anything to happen to you."

As much as she did was right. Exactly as much as she did. He had a lovable way of wanting children when she wanted to have them, and hating them when she couldn't have them.

"Nothing's going to happen to me.... Do you believe me?"

"You know something ... I do. Really do. Come here.... I love you. Happy Birthday."

Having dared, they then put the mountain behind them and coasted for a while. From one unreality to another. Mount Pregnancy to Disneyworld. Their feet never touched the ground.

Coasting, they rose again. The ride, called Space Mountain, was a roller coaster in a gargantuan enclosure. They had hesitated at first, but what the hell, they'd faced worse together; they were mountain climbers now—another mountain shouldn't stop them. As high as they were riding, their car went higher and faster, hurling them side to side, a little too rough for her.

They came down. They continued south. He complained about the speed limits. She began to complain about her right leg. It was the roller-coaster ride.

For two weeks, they blamed Space Mountain as

the pain, centered around her knee, got worse. She had also missed her period, but she knew she wasn't pregnant—pregnancy only happened to normal girls who didn't have any problems. She couldn't even get rid of a sore leg. . . . It was a gentle reminder of the sorry state of her body. When the pain became unbearable, Ted insisted on taking her to a doctor in Miami, who examined her at the hospital and said it was a blood clot and that she should be on medication immediately. She was ready to hop back to Memorial on one leg; nothing was going to keep her in any other hospital.

Ted moved quickly, too quickly for her mother: she was supposed to meet them at the Miami airport; Ted would put the two of them on the next plane to New York; then he would drive back with her father. Her mother was so nervous that she packed two suitcases of appropriate clothing and then took two different suitcases with her. One of them was filled with shoes and mothballs. The other was empty.

As Angela lay on a stretcher in the airport, she played an old game: Angela, if you make believe you're pregnant, it won't be so scary.

There was a seat for her mother, a seat for her, and a seat in between, courtesy of the airline, for her leg. There it lay, a thing of its own. They both stared at it. They looked away, at clouds, at people, and returned to it. It wasn't swollen. It wasn't discolored. It wasn't hot. Over it, they spoke softly.

"Could you be pregnant?"

"Technically, I could be."

"Why?"

166

"I want my own child."

"Why do you do these things! . . . You know you'll get caught!"

Her mother saw it differently from anybody else: she was a wayward girl.

The gathering of the Ambrosia clan at Kennedy brought Angela back to reality: the only thing she was carrying was a blood clot, and that clot carried with it the threat of another pulmonary embolism. She was taken off the plane at Kennedy by wheelchair and rushed to Memorial.

Dowling was on vacation. The doctor who saw her gave her pain-killers. She asked: "If I'm pregnant, can this hurt my pregnancy?" He answered: "You're not pregnant."

They drew blood gases from an artery in her wrist. Or tried. Then they tried the other wrist. They went back and forth four or five times, and by the time they were done, her veins had blown up to the size of golf balls, two black-and-blue purple lumps the size of actual golf balls. She had to press her wrists together, and the sight and the sensation made her sick and she began to have convulsions. They wheeled in an electrocardiograph machine, and the needle went crazy. So did she. "If I'm pregnant, can this hurt my pregnancy?" "You're not pregnant."

The swelling went down in a half-hour. They gave her tranquilizers and she slept. She woke as they were taking her down to have her leg X-rayed. She was beginning to feel like their prisoner. She asked for a shield to protect her pelvic area, "just in case." They refused. "You're not pregnant."

"Then why don't I have my period?" she began demanding.

"Now try not to be upset."

She braced herself. She was trying.

"You're going through menopause."

"Meno—At my age! Are you crazy?"

"Try not to upset yourself. I know it's very difficult at your age, but it's from all the medication you've taken. Sooner or later, all those drugs work on a body this way. We think it's the end of your periods. So don't worry about it. You're going through an early menopause."

Don't worry about it! A dried-up prune at twenty-four and he was telling her not to worry about it! She said it out loud to him. She told him they were all crazy. She told them she thought she was pregnant.

To satisfy her—to silence her—they gave her a pregnancy test. It came back negative.

They couldn't find anything wrong with her leg. She had come to them a young girl with a blood clot and a false pregnancy; she was going away from them sterile. They gave her Darvon—Darvon, which she had had so much trouble getting off of—for the pain, which still existed, and sent her limping "merrily on her way."

Camille called to find out how Angela was feeling. She was a little nauseated, a little warm, and crying at the drop of a hat. She told Camille that she still thought she might be pregnant. "You're not pregnant." "You know, Camille, there is the slightest chance—" Camille interrupted her. "You're not pregnant, you're a fool!" They screamed at each other and she hung up on her beloved Camille. She was thirteen again, and getting messages from her body again, and no one, not even her sister, would believe her.

Whatever he believed, Ted never uttered those three words *You're not pregnant*. Twice, on his way out the door in the morning, Angela handed him large urine specimens, which he dutifully took to Memorial, to the same doctors—with what words of explanation or apology, she didn't want to know. The results kept coming back negative.

They were having a new couch delivered. Angela excused herself and went into the bathroom to vomit. As she emerged, for the second time, hair and teeth brushed, the man in charge greeted her with "Lady, you're pregnant!" She said, "You just hit the jackpot. . . . The doctors say I'm not." "Lady, I remember that same look on my wife's face. You're pregnant!"

She believed him. But how was she going to convince the world by telling them her furniture deliverer said so? She was vomiting with impressive frequency and she had a little fever, so they started treating her for the flu. She gave Ted one more urine sample. She promised it was the last time, but she was probably lying.

Memorial does not deal with many pregnancies. They have no obstetrics department. The same doctor kept giving the same nurse the urine of the same person—Angela Ambrosia Rubel—with orders to do an A-Z test, which is a good test in an advanced stage of pregnancy—"like your twenty-fourth month, for example!"—but not reliable for detecting early pregnancies. Tired of Angela and her urine, the nurse ignored the doctor's instructions and ran a gravindex, a test for early pregnancy.

The phone rang. It was Dr. Friel, the gynecologist. "You are pregnant."

For the first time in her life, Angela was normal. "I was like everyone else. I didn't feel unique.... I felt like everyone. Everyone else was immortal. Me, too. I used to compare myself with other pregnant women. 'You're pregnant? Me, too.' 'You're throwing up? Me, too.' 'You're sick as a dog? Me, too.' I thought: Now I can't die. I have life in me. I'm immortal.

"It was wonderful."

*S*he put on weight quickly, so her stomach would look rounder. She decorated the little roundness with maternity clothes. She saw to it that everyone—a bus driver she'd never seen before, an usher in a darkened movie theatre—treated her like a pregnant woman. She insisted those close to her treat her condition, in every way, like a normal pregnancy. She warned the doctors to treat it only like a healthy pregnancy. "I don't want to hear..." A long list followed.

Her mother, the woman who had had three children of her own, carried on as if she'd never seen a pregnancy before. "It's a miracle," she would repeat as she rubbed her daughter's stomach, "a miracle.

There's a baby in here." She couldn't believe that the child she'd come so close to losing so many times was going to—could—have a child of her own.

She was entering her third month of pregnancy and feeling no pain. It worried her. From the beginning she'd felt the adhesions in her womb stretching—so many operations, so many scars. Now she was comfortable. At one point, her blood pressure had gone down to 70/60, but it was up again and she felt fine. She was relieved that her breasts weren't as sore as they had been, but they weren't as firm, either. Still, when she looked in the mirror, she saw someone about to become a mother. She told herself to stop worrying.

Easter Sunday her family gathered at her apartment. To celebrate the resurrection and the life. Her parents were returning to Florida in the morning. Camille and Tony, Philip and Johanna came and went from their own lives. A moment of panic—had she ever intended so complete a cut-off?—preceded the dawn. . . . She was no longer any-one's little girl.

She woke up in a pool of blood. She was dreaming. Her parents had left yesterday . . . she was nervous. She was dreaming. She was sweating . . . there was nothing to be afraid of . . . if only she could wake up. Turn over. Sit up a little. Up. She wasn't dreaming. She woke up in a pool of blood.

She pushed Ted. "I'm bleeding." She shook him.

"I'm bleeding." She shook and shook him. "Ted, wake up, I'm bleeding!" When he woke, when he saw, he panicked. "Get dressed, I'll take you to the hospital." He was up and moving. "Get dressed." She had never seen him panic before, and it frightened her even more. "Ted, I'm afraid to get up. . . . What if I hemorrhage more?" "Get dressed! You can dress yourself!" She watched him changing pajama tops and thought she'd better get dressed. "What are you doing up?" "You told me to get up. . . . " "You shouldn't be on your feet. Lie down. . . . I'll dress you." He dressed her in a pair of shorts and a sweater. In April. She leaned against the dresser; he went to get their coats.

She met herself unexpectedly in the mirror and refused to turn away. This was a showdown. "You loser, you loser, you thought you could do it but you're nothing but a loser. You've always been a loser and you'll always be a loser—you'd be better off dead!" She stared. "Don't," he said as he draped a coat over her shoulders and wrapped it around her. "Easy, now."

It was pouring. And freezing. While Ted struggled with the limited visibility, she clutched at her stomach and joined the rhythm of the windshield wipers. "You loser, you loser." It became a comforting chant. "You loser, you loser, you'll always be a loser." It got louder, over the defroster and the heater and the rain. "Loser . . . loser . . . " Ted exploded: it wasn't true and he didn't want to hear it. She woke for the second time that night. Ted was right; what was she saying? "Ted, am I going to lose the baby?" "You're not going to lose it, Ange. We're going to work as hard as we've ever worked, and you're not going to lose it." "My baby," she said, "my baby," in her own slow rhythm, "my baby," expressionless, as tears streamed down her cheeks and she rocked herself into a trance.

When they removed her from the car, Ted saw that she was covered with blood. A doctor ran alongside the wheelchair asking questions, but the answer was always "My baby." Ted, thinking for her, did what she would otherwise have done, requested a priest. They couldn't find one.

It wasn't until she was in the examining room that she realized she wasn't at Memorial, but at Lenox Hill Hospital. That there would be no Dowling to take charge. That she was a stranger in the hands of strangers. It didn't matter. "Save my baby."

She hadn't lost it yet. If she could hold on to it another twenty-four hours—and if the bleeding stopped—she might keep it. Ted hadn't lied. Perhaps.

She spent four anxious days in the hospital. The bleeding stopped after two of them, but sharp, barely bearable pain took its place. She refused pain-killers for fear the baby might fall asleep and fall out. The examinations and the cautious presentiments continued.

The "hands of strangers" were kind. They brought her a Bible; they held her hands. They rubbed her back and rubbed her stomach till she fell asleep. They worked overtime without charge. They didn't leave her alone.

Ted brought a book of babies' names. It took awhile, but soon they joked, giggled a lot, decided it had to be a boy, and named him Gregory. It was good to see her laughing; he tickled her—once. "Don't do that!" she screamed, and got up to check herself and there was a trickle of blood. "You animal," she said, "did you have to do that? I had stopped, and now I'm bleeding again!" Even as she said it, she knew. It wasn't the tickle. But the blame had to go somewhere. Her shoulders were too stooped, her constitution too weak, for her to take it.

For four days, she had forgotten about immortality, about normality, about herself; all she thought about was her baby. On the fifth day she lost it.

Her cervix was open. She had passed the placenta. . . . The baby was dead inside her. She wailed, and then she keened. She was too dry to cry.

She would need a complete D & C in the morning. They would also have to take a lot of blood. She might have an infection. She could foreseeably have leukemia again. There was a lot to consider—they would take it one step at a time. Would she like her psychiatrist? Yes. A priest? Yes. Dowling? Not right now. Tonight, leave her alone with Ted and her faith.

As they took her into the operating room, an infant was crying. Half asleep, she promised: Mommy's not going to kill you. When she came out of the anesthesia, she picked up where she had left off: "Is it a boy or a girl?" She rephrased her question: "Is it alive?" She went back to sleep with the truth.

She was home in time for Mother's Day. And Ted's birthday, which coincided with it. Her blood— unaffected, unchanged by pregnancy—was absolutely normal. So, to their scant consolation, was her miscarriage. Normal miscarriage. It never struck them as a cruel contradiction of terms. They found in it something positive to cling to. For the future.

They weren't hiding or packing away the maternity clothes, the toys, the baby books; they were saving them. She clutched a stuffed animal, a bear with a button nose and pink fur. "Ted . . . they'll never give me another chance."

*D*owling told her how sorry he was. But he wasn't. He was her custodian and he was relieved. Glad that it happened as early as it had. He didn't want anything to interfere with her "progress."

She had gone through her crisis, beginning to end, without him. That would be a good thing to bear in mind for the future. He marveled at how strong she was and waited for her to fold. She saw to it that their sessions were strictly business.

He couldn't tell her that he would soon be leaving—Memorial and New York. She received a printed announcement. "Monroe D. Dowling, Jr., M.D., will be . . . and thereafter . . . Lincoln, Nebraska."

"*I* made a good trade for that pillow of mine. I got a wonderful man. Who holds me before I go to sleep, hours before. Who rubs my back or pats my head. Or sings me to sleep. Who thinks I'm beautiful, even when I'm bald, and tells me so. Who praises as he pats and bolsters as he rubs. Who fluffs me up. . . .

"No one ever made me feel so near normal. He treats me as a person—not as an invalid or a terminal case, but a person. As soon as anyone else knows what I have, I become my disease and I come second. With Ted, my blood is just a part of me the way my hand or a rib is a part of me. When I'm sick, he does what anyone would do for someone they love, and doesn't keep count. When I'm well, we're even."

She doesn't ask for material things too much, because she knows she'll get them. He's a man who knows how to say no to her but has never denied her anything. From the day they returned from their honeymoon to the day, a year ago, when he became the director of his department and could pay for something besides her medical bills, "He somehow managed, and mostly went without.

"So, I'm a very lucky person—I lived long enough to see things fall into place. . . . So many young people died too early and did not. I still bite the ears off the chocolate bunny my mother sends me every Easter. My mother gave birth to me and Dowling gave me life. Ted showed me how to live it. To this day, I can't get over staying out late and not having to answer to

176

anyone—just having fun with my husband ... the feeling I have of still being on my honeymoon ... no longer being afraid of the dark. But just as he doesn't put me on crutches, I don't put him on a pedestal. I'm fully aware that he has to be one hell of a man to have me ... but, let's face it, I'm one hell of a woman. Together, we've had a hell of a lot of perfect days."

S he was there to say goodbye to Dowling. She was still an outpatient, but not his. There to see her past leaving, there to forget about the past. "The only times I ever recall—moments I remember like a rich taste, or a good swim—are all the good times you gave me. No one understands that. Not even you."

"I have only one problem—staying alive."
Her blood does unpredictable things. She had just got out of bed. She was standing over the bathroom sink when her heart began to swell. She lost her breath, felt her chest about to burst violently open.

It was a double pulmonary embolism. Two blood clots had passed through her heart and one had lodged in each lung. Had they stopped at her heart, she would have died.

Unpredictable things. She had just got out of bed. She felt faint, feverish without a fever. Taking no chances, Dr. Reich told Ted to bring her in immediately for blood tests.

177

Her white count had shot up to 80,000. The Philadelphia chromosome was present. She was in danger, but not grave danger. She consented to take the chemo for a week or two. The white count returned to a safe 5,000; the forbidding chromosome stayed. And stays.

"The leukemia feels like dirt in my veins. There's no reason to believe that it won't happen again. One of these times stands to be the last. Each time now, I wonder: Is this it?"

There is always that strain on their marriage. In the meantime, she sees herself married forever. "We consider the two of us a family. He treats the Ambrosias like friends who always drop by at dinnertime. We both treat my in-laws like in-laws."

*T*hey like every day. They like seasons and they like fresh air. She particularly likes running into it. And they like a local Chinese restaurant where he taught her how to eat with chopsticks when she couldn't stomach herself . . . and the owner calls her Angel-Luck.

A NOTE ON THE TYPE

This book was set on the VIP in Century Expanded, a type designed in 1894 by Linn Boyd Benton (1844–1932). Benton cut Century Expanded in response to Theodore De Vinne's request for an attractive, easy-to-read type face to fit the narrow columns of his *Century Magazine.* Early in the nineteen hundreds Morris Fuller Benton updated and improved Century in several versions for his father's American Type Founders Company. Century remains the only American type face cut before 1910 still widely in use today.

Composed by Publishers Phototype, Incorporated, Carlstadt, New Jersey. Printed and bound by The Haddon Craftsmen, Scranton, Pennsylvania.

Typography and binding design by Virginia Tan.